PIL_TES
FOR
BREAST CANCER SURVIVORS

A Guide to Recovery, Healing, and Wellness

Naomi Aaronson, MA, OTR/L, CHT, CPI, CET

Ann Marie Turo, OTR/L

demosHEALTH
NEW YORK

Visit our website at www.demoshealth.com

ISBN: 978-1-936303-57-1
e-book ISBN: 978-1-617051-95-1

Acquisitions Editor: Julia Pastore
Compositor: diacriTech

Medical information provided by Demos Health, in the absence of a visit with a health care professional, must be considered as an educational service only. This book is not designed to replace a physician's independent judgment about the appropriateness or risks of a procedure or therapy for a given patient. Our purpose is to provide you with information that will help you make your own health care decisions.

The information and opinions provided here are believed to be accurate and sound, based on the best judgment available to the authors, editors, and publisher, but readers who fail to consult appropriate health authorities assume the risk of injuries. The publisher is not responsible for errors or omissions. The editors and publisher welcome any reader to report to the publisher any discrepancies or inaccuracies noticed.

Library of Congress Cataloging-in-Publication Data

Aaronson, Naomi, author.
  Pilates for breast cancer survivors : a guide to recovery, healing, and wellness / Naomi Aaronson, Ann Marie Turo.
    p. ; cm.
  Includes bibliographical references and index.
  ISBN 978-1-936303-57-1—ISBN 978-1-61705-195-1 (e-book)
  I. Turo, Ann Marie, author. II. Title.
  [DNLM: 1. Breast Neoplasms—rehabilitation—Popular Works. 2. Breathing Exercises—Popular Works. 3. Exercise Movement Techniques—Popular Works. 4. Relaxation Therapy—Popular Works. WP 870]

  RC271.Y63
  616.99'44906—dc23

                          2014020932

Special discounts on bulk quantities of Demos Health books are available to corporations, professional associations, pharmaceutical companies, health care organizations, and other qualifying groups. For details, please contact:

Special Sales Department
Demos Medical Publishing, LLC
11 West 42nd Street, 15th Floor
New York, NY 10036
Phone: 800-532-8663 or 212-683-0072
Fax: 212-941-7842
E-mail: specialsales@demosmedical.com

Printed in the United States of America by Bang Printing.
14 15 16 17 18 / 5 4 3 2 1

FOR

BREAST CANCER
SURVIVORS

Date: 10/6/15

616.99449 AAR
Aaronson, Naomi,
Pilates for breast cancer
survivors :a guide to

This book is dedicated to Beth Mast, an occupational therapist and Pilates practitioner who has used Pilates to recover from breast cancer and who is now using Pilates on her journey through living with metastatic cancer. Beth says that, "Pilates can be done by even the weakest." It was the only exercise that she could tolerate after going through chemotherapy and becoming increasingly anemic, unable to stand even to brush her teeth.

Learning to live with cancer is an art, not a science. Each person must find her own way, in her own style. What is important to realize is that a way can be found regardless of the circumstances and prospects.

—*Jane E. Brody*

Contents

Preface

Ann Marie's Journey through Breast Cancer

I was always a person who exercised, took a whole arsenal of vitamins, read everything on health and fitness, and ate correctly. As an occupational therapist, I prided myself on being up on my health and well-being. So when I got the diagnosis of breast cancer, I was in shock. How could this be? But in January of 1991, my doctor found a tiny lump the size of a pea in my left breast. My breast cancer journey began.

My mind was telling me: They read the wrong pathology report: **DENIAL.** I took care of myself how could this be: **ANGER.** If I could just have my health back, I'll never stand in front of the microwave again and will only eat organic foods: **BARGAINING.** There were days I couldn't dress myself, or days that I would put the same clothing on that I had dumped on the chair the night before: **DEPRESSION.** These stages should sound familiar to every person who has been diagnosed with a life threatening illness or disease. Many people will go through at least one or all of the Kübler-Ross stages of grief.

I was lucky. I received a lumpectomy/partial mastectomy and clean margins were reached.

In 2001, eleven years after my first diagnosis, breast cancer came knocking at my door again in the left breast. At that moment, I felt a sense of acceptance as I knew what I needed to do, but immediately, I moved again into the denial stage. I told my doctor that "I was here today for my yearly mammogram and not for surgery." The cycle of anger, bargaining, and depression repeated itself.

When you are diagnosed with a disease such as cancer, your life changes from that moment on. You begin to think about your future, and whether you will be here one year from now. You also think about what is important to you and your family, and what life really means to you. You make decisions based on the information that is available to you. You think about what you are willing to endure. The what ifs and the if nots play around in your head. But each of us is different and will make different treatment decisions. I made mine based on what I felt would provide me the best chance of survival and quality of life.

In 2002, three months after another partial mastectomy, I decided to enroll in Pilates reformer training (a reformer is a piece of resistance exercise equipment designed by Joseph Pilates). I had been trained in mat Pilates in 2001, but felt this was a natural next step. I got the OK from my surgeon and moved forward. When I look back on it today, it wasn't the best decision. I was not completely healed, had poor endurance, left shoulder tightness, and my scapula was nowhere to be found! My proprioception (awareness of my own body in space) and kinesthetic awareness (my ability to sense movement) was so poor that I had no clue where my left arm was or what it was doing. The training was tough, but I kept on telling myself, "If I got through breast cancer, I could get through anything." I don't recommend that you start with reformer training, but Pilates is an excellent way to heal. Pilates was the best thing for me then. It helped me regain my strength and the confidence to navigate the world after undergoing life changing surgery and treatment. The deep breathing along with the specific Pilates exercises in this book helped me to focus and relax, as well as stretch my tight chest, side, and back muscles. Finally, Pilates offered me the opportunity to regain control over a body that had betrayed me as well as providing a safe and nurturing space to relax and focus on healing and recovery.

That saying, "It's the journey not the destination," is so true. Pilates has come full circle for me in the healing process, as now I am sharing this modality with my patients and other health professionals. In 2004, I opened Integrated Mind & Body, a health and wellness studio, and completed my yoga, Pilates, and Reiki training. It was important to me to offer a range of mind-body therapies in addition to traditional rehabilitation techniques in order to holistically and optimally meet patient and client goals.

Naomi and I met at the Cotting Connection Conference in Boston in October 2007. The medical community, patients, and vendors were brought together to learn about some of the new and innovative treatments in the area of breast cancer treatment and rehabilitation. Naomi had a vendor table set up with her breast cancer CDs, courses, and books on exercise for breast cancer recovery and had presented a session on exercise. We are both occupational therapists with an emphasis upon improving function and wellness as well as fitness professionals, so we had a lot in common. We discussed doing a course together one day, exchanged business cards, and went our separate ways.

In December 2007, Naomi contacted me and asked if she could interview me for an article in *Advance for Occupational Therapy Practitioners* that was entitled "Movement Towards Healing." We then decided to integrate our passion for the healing properties of movement and the power of occupational therapy to rehabilitate cancer survivors. We formed a company named Integrated Rehab and Fitness with the goal of educating other rehabilitation and fitness professionals. In September 2008, we presented our first course

"Breast Cancer Rehabilitation Using a Pilates Based Approach" in Natick, Massachusetts. Since then, we have spread the word to therapists and other rehabilitation professionals about the benefits of Pilates for breast cancer survivors. Our CD *Return to Life: Breast Cancer Recovery Using a Pilates Based Approach* is available for continuing education at home. We are excited to be able to bring our information to breast cancer survivors throughout the world through publication of this book!

Our goal with this book is to help you heal, regain control, strength, and confidence, and be able to perform daily living tasks more easily, whether or not you've ever done Pilates before. We've provided various programs and modifications so that no matter where you are in treatment, what side effects you may be experiencing, or your general fitness level, you will be able to find exercises you can do comfortably and safely and achieve benefit. However, to attain wellness, exercise alone is not enough; you must adopt habits and behaviors that promote an improved quality of life. Wellness is a lifelong journey: a process of growing. Unfortunately, cancer treatment has some long-lasting effects. In the final section of the book, we've included ways to deal with issues such as chemo brain, sleep deprivation, and peripheral neuropathy.

Throughout the book, we've also included the experiences of other survivors who have used Pilates as part of their journey to health. We hope you'll find their reflections and insights helpful:

Beth Mast, who is an occupational therapist as well as a Pilates instructor, underwent 16 months of treatment, including a double mastectomy, breast implants, chemotherapy, and radiation, and used Pilates daily. It helped her battle scar tissue, maintain strength and range of motion in her arms, address sensory issues such as sensitivity to touch, and move through menopause.

Nicole T. felt pain in her chest immediately after surgery, and was unable to sit up without assistance for two weeks after undergoing a mastectomy and breast reconstruction with saline implants. She had difficulty raising her arms, but this got easier over time. The more she did, the better she felt. The repetition was important to her. She warns other women beginning a Pilates routine that you will receive a lot of information at once and may not be able to absorb all of it. So you may have to re-visit the basics throughout your recovery. She found that it felt good to be in the company of people who understood her condition. When she finished her Pilates exercise sessions, Nicole left feeling loose and optimistic.

Grace T. had bilateral preventive mastectomies followed by silicone implant breast reconstruction. She had tenderness in both shoulders, tightness across her chest, and weakness in her arms. She felt beaten up, tired, sensitive, weak, and bloated. Gaining back strength and flexibility contributed to her confidence and reconnection with her body. This helped her to feel better emotionally. "Pilates is a great way to recover, as it seems meant for people recovering from illness as well as getting back to physical fitness."

Sharon B. had a lumpectomy with sentinel node biopsy, followed by a second surgery for clean margins, radiation, and chemotherapy. She experienced pain and muscle tightness at her scar sites and limited range of shoulder motion. Exercises such as Wall Angels, Swimming, and Scapula Protraction and Retraction have helped her recover.

Nancy M. had a lumpectomy and radiation. The Pilates exercises that stretched her side and strengthened her core helped her the most. She encourages others to start a program of Pilates immediately. "Do not wait until the situation has progressed to a point where your body has become rigid from under movement. Pilates integrates well with breast cancer recovery, as the focus is on thoughtful movement or movement with intent."

Bonnie O. is a personal trainer who knows how important movement is. She experienced surgery and chemotherapy. Immediately after surgery her body felt like it had been hit by a truck, and in the weeks and months following she primarily felt tightness in the chest and shoulders, as if a belt was buckled tightly around her ribcage. She developed cording in her right arm, where she had 16 lymph nodes removed, and a frozen shoulder. Exercising regularly, focusing on regaining flexibility, and keeping her core strong aided her recovery.

We've made it our mission to educate others about the benefits of an integrated approach to rehabilitation and recovery. We hope this book will help you achieve maximum wellness, now and throughout your journey living life after cancer. This is your action plan for health!

Acknowledgments

Alexander Gence for providing his expertise in photographing models.

Our Pilates models Diana Laird and Cheryl Lanava Gence for their patience while undergoing numerous takes of the photos.

Our brave breast cancer survivors who were willing to help others through their cancer journey: Beth Mast, Grace T., Sharon B., Nicole T., Nancy M., and Bonnie O.

PART I

Introduction to Pilates for Breast Cancer

Why Pilates for Breast Cancer?

Pilates is a gentle form of exercise that engages the mind, body, and spirit. The various exercises in Pilates help to develop muscular flexibility and strength while increasing metabolism and promoting lymphatic, respiratory, and circulatory function. They improve balance and coordination and will also help you to "get centered" and relax. Pilates is able to meet you where you are, and it can be done throughout your life and wherever you are, even while seated. For these reasons, it is an excellent approach to healing for breast cancer survivors.

Pilates was first developed by Joseph Pilates to strengthen muscles, increase flexibility, and improve overall health. It is a mixture of yoga, martial arts, and gymnastics. He first taught his method as "Contrology," a mash-up of Eastern and Western philosophies and techniques, to a small group of devoted teachers and students in the United States after emigrating from Germany following World War I. Years later, in the 1950s, Pilates used his method to rehabilitate dancers at his studio in New York City without receiving much recognition for his method.

One of Pilates's first protégés was Eve Gentry. She was rehabilitated by Joseph Pilates after a radical mastectomy. She was able to regain full use of her arm and torso, which is remarkable since all of her lymph nodes and chest muscles, as well as breast tissue, were removed with this procedure. Doctors could not believe the success that she had obtained with the Joseph Pilates method. Pilates was a man ahead of the times. Fortunately, research is now being conducted that documents the benefits of Pilates for breast cancer recovery.

What are the benefits of Pilates?

Beth Mast has used Pilates daily throughout her breast cancer journey. It is a form of exercise that is always available to her, even on really bad days. Here are the benefits Beth has found with her Pilates practice:

1. You can do Pilates in many different positions: supine (on the back), prone (on the stomach), side lying, standing, or seated.

2. The exercises and equipment can be modified for any level.

3. You will be able to use the affected arm(s) more easily and naturally since Pilates is a whole body exercise system that includes the arms and legs in the movements.

4. The principles help you to live in the moment by keeping you focused on moving properly, with control, and without momentum.

5. Deep rib cage breathing and the multidimensional breathing patterns help to ease tension, foster lymphatic drainage, and stretch tight areas affected by scars.

6. Pilates provides a gentle introduction or reintroduction to exercise.

7. Pilates increases muscle strength, especially in the back of the shoulders and middle back where you need it after breast cancer surgery.

8. Pilates increases your ability to perform activities of daily living (ADL) as you build core strength allowing you to roll over and move from different positions more easily.

9. Pilates improves muscle proprioception and kinesthesia, often lost after surgery where nerves and muscles may have been inadvertently cut.

10. Pilates strengthens the transverse abdominis: a muscle that is very important for back stability and strength after a TRAM flap (transverse rectus abdominis myocutaneous) or DIEP flap (deep inferior epigastric perforator) breast reconstruction procedure.

11. Pilates can help with bladder control problems such as stress incontinence, a common complication of menopause. Many treatments for breast cancer can induce menopause in women who are not yet menopausal. Pilates helps by strengthening the pelvic floor muscles, which are the muscles responsible for bladder control.

12. Pilates takes the focus off of the damaged areas of your body and what you can't do and reinforces what you can do. You'll appreciate all of the movement your body is capable of, no matter how "small" or limited at first, and its capacity to heal.

The "American Cancer Society Guidelines on Nutrition and Physical Activity for Cancer Survivors" recommend that breast cancer survivors should avoid inactivity and return as soon as possible to normal activities after surgery and during radiation and adjuvant treatment (chemotherapy, hormone therapy, and/or targeted therapy). They recommend regular physical activity, strength training at least twice a week, and to aim for 150 minutes of exercise per week.

Physical activity offers other benefits for breast cancer survivors, such as the following.

- Boosts positive mood

- Improves physical condition and movement

- Improves body image

- Increases sexuality

- Decreases depression

- Decreases fatigue

- Maintains bone health

We know that exercise is good for us. We just need to start somewhere and feel safe. Pilates is a gentle, safe place to begin.

What does the research say?

The first study on the benefits of Pilates for breast cancer survivors was completed by physical therapists in 2008. It was a pilot study with only four participants, so the conclusions we can draw from this study are limited. They found that Pilates increased the flexibility of the affected arm after a 12-week program during which participants exercised three times a week.

Another study, done in 2010, examined the effects of Pilates exercises on functional capacity, flexibility, fatigue, depression, and quality of life in female breast cancer patients. Pilates was performed three times a week for eight weeks. After participation in the Pilates exercises, improvements were noted in the subjects' levels of fatigue, flexibility, quality of life, and performance on a six-minute walk test. This study proved that Pilates was safe and effective for breast cancer survivors.

The most recent study, published in 2012, found that after 12 weeks of Pilates 13 participants improved their shoulder and neck flexibility. Improvements were noted in quality of life, body image, and mood. Although volume increased on the affected arm (a sign of lymphedema), one must note that this program did not modify the exercises for the class and that the sessions increased in frequency over the 12-week period.

What are the issues faced by breast cancer survivors?

You have done your best to follow your medical treatment plan, but there may be some lingering physical, emotional, or cognitive issues. Breast cancer surgery involves removal of tissue and lymph nodes from the breast region. Due to the large area that the breast tissue covers, you may experience difficulty performing daily life activities, working, and caring for your children. In addition, chemotherapy and radiation can cause a variety of side effects such as fatigue and nausea.

Here are some things to look out for during and after your treatment. An occupational therapist or physical therapist will be able to help you regain your functional abilities, make recommendations for assistive devices, or train you in alternative methods of performing your life tasks. The good news is that rehabilitation, including the Pilates program outlined in this book, can help you get stronger, regain function, and alleviate these side effects.

1. **Lymphedema** is one of the most common conditions faced by survivors after removal of lymph nodes and/or radiation. Early recognition is important for treatment. Although there is a significantly lower rate of lymphedema for sentinel node biopsies (the node that is the first to receive lymphatic drainage is called the sentinel node), one is still at risk. Thus, you are at risk for lymphedema both for axillary lymph node dissections as well as sentinel node biopsies. Know what type of surgery you had, whether lymph nodes were removed, and any precautions to follow. Be sure to educate yourself about strategies to decrease risk.

   Lymphedema is characterized by a feeling of fullness, achiness, decreased movement, tightness, heaviness, or tingling in the chest wall, arm, shoulder, neck, trunk, breast, and/or hand due to abnormal accumulation of protein rich fluid. You may notice that jewelry is tight or that your clothes don't fit properly. Lymphedema is the buildup of fluid in soft body tissues when the lymph system is damaged or blocked from breast cancer surgery and/or radiation. The lymphatic system is responsible for removing waste products, fighting infection, and regulating body fluid balance. After the surgery, your lymphatic system may lose its ability to perform these functions, causing a "traffic jam" or buildup of lymphatic fluid.

   If you note the above, ask your doctor for a referral to a certified lymphedema therapist who can perform a special type of massage to reduce the traffic jam and divert this build up to other "roads" in your body. Your doctor may recommend bandaging or wearing a special garment that applies pressure to the arm, as well as a glove called a gauntlet, on a daily basis.

2. **Loss of range of motion and strength in the affected arm(s)**. Since there is so much loss of tissue, you can experience decreased flexibility in the chest, trunk, and shoulder regions, impairing your ability to perform daily life tasks such as dressing, making your bed, and reaching for items.

3. **Pain** can be an issue after surgery that can affect the neck, shoulder, chest, and arm, thus impairing mobility and strength. Postmastectomy pain syndrome (PMPS) is chronic pain that is thought to be caused by nerve damage after surgery. You may experience burning or shooting pain in the underarm, arm, shoulder, or chest wall. Drain sites may be painful as well.

4. **Scar tissue** may cause tightening under the arm and around the incisions, drain sites, and reconstruction sites. Scars can be itchy and painful. Your therapist can show you how to perform scar massage or recommend silicone pads to decrease scar thickness and redness.

5. **Axillary web syndrome or "cording"** may be seen soon after lymph node removal but can occur any time after having lymph nodes removed. You may notice an inability to straighten your elbow and bring your arm out to the side. There is usually a visible, tight cord from your armpit down the arm, and pain in the armpit or when bringing your arm out to the side.

6. **"Chemo brain"** refers to the cognitive changes caused by chemotherapy such as changes in attention, concentration, working memory, and executive function. Prevalence rates can range from 17% to 75% in individuals with breast cancer. Perceived cognitive difficulties are more commonly reported than objective measurements from testing, so be sure to let your provider know if you are experiencing cognitive challenges.

Nicole T. felt that chemo brain was the hardest thing to deal with after treatment. It was something that she was not warned about, so she was surprised and unprepared for it. She was unable to remember things and speak the way that she had before undergoing chemo treatments. She had difficulty remembering how to do the Pilates exercises that she had to perform at home.

It is important to let health care providers know that you have cognitive challenges such as difficulty multitasking or remembering simple things. Ask your doctor for a referral to an occupational therapist who can evaluate your cognitive functioning and recommend some simple adaptations to your daily routine. Medication may also prove beneficial if warranted.

7. **Chemotherapy-induced peripheral neuropathy** (CIPN) is damage to and lack of function of the peripheral nerves—the motor, sensory, and autonomic nerves that connect the brain and spinal cord to the rest of the body. It results from chemotherapy drugs and can cause a lack of sensation in the hands and feet. There may be numbness, decreased sensitivity to heat and cold, decreased feeling of light touch, decreased position sense, tingling, or pain from drugs such as Taxol, carboplatin, cisplatin, or vinorelbine. There can be a high risk for falls, so caution when standing, walking, or running is advised. To determine if you may be experiencing CIPN, ask yourself: Do I drop things? Do I have difficulty walking? Do I have difficulty climbing stairs? Do the sensations interfere with my ability to work or perform daily activities? (Cooking, cleaning, dressing, writing, and typing may be affected.)

   The National Comprehensive Cancer Network Panelists agreed that transcutaneous electrical nerve stimulation (TENS) can be a helpful adjuvant therapy for CIPN in those with contraindications or for whom pain medication is ineffective. Also, acupuncture may be considered an adjunct option in treating patients who do not respond to medication. In addition, occupational therapists or physical therapists can prove invaluable by recommending alternative ways to strengthen the affected areas and modify daily activities with special equipment. Since Pilates can be performed in seated or supine positions, it is a safe form of exercise to build strength without worry of falling.

8. **Bone metastasis** is the spread of cancer cells from the initial area of cancer through the bloodstream to the bones. This can damage the bones, making them weaker and more likely to break. Bone metastases are a common cause of pain. The most common sites of bone metastases are the upper arms and legs, pelvis, rib cage, skull, and spine. Bone metastases can wear away portions of the bone, leaving small holes. Thus, the bone becomes more vulnerable to fracture. One needs to be careful with exercises that can increase your risk of fractures. The seated Pilates program would be the safest and most recommended program for you to participate in to decrease your risk of falling. It would be best to work with a therapist who specializes in breast cancer and knows how to modify the exercises for you if your breast cancer has metastasized to the bone.

9. **Osteoporosis or osteopenia** is thinning of bone mass and density. You may have a higher risk of breaking a bone. The bones most likely to fracture are in the spine, wrist, and hip. Risk factors include getting older, being small and thin, a family history of osteoporosis, and low bone mass, or osteopenia. Chemotherapy and hormonal treatments such as Arimedex, Aromasin, or Femara, as well as ovarian shutdown, can contribute to bone loss. Be sure to check with your medical provider about a dual-energy x-ray absorptiometry (DEXA) scan to get a baseline measure of your bone density. Make sure to get enough calcium. Usually, 1200 mg of calcium and 600 IU of vitamin D per day is recommended for women over 50. Weight-bearing exercises that put weight on your joints, such as walking, dancing, lifting weights, and the standing program in Pilates, also build bone strength. Please be sure to check with your medical provider before beginning any exercise plan.

10. **Cancer related fatigue (CRF).** Approximately 58% to 94% of breast cancer patients experience CRF. It is the number one problem with cancer survivorship, and is a persistent state of tiredness related to cancer or cancer treatment. Women who undergo surgery, radiation, and chemotherapy experience the most fatigue. It can affect your sense of well-being, your ability to work and perform ADL, and your relationships with family and friends. Aerobic exercise such as walking, biking, and Pilates has been found to help with this fatigue. In addition, anemia or low red blood cell count impairs the body's ability to carry oxygen. Be sure to know your blood counts to see if you are anemic during chemotherapy, as you may need to scale back your exercise.

11. **Cardiotoxicity** is damage to the heart from chemotherapy treatment. Thirty-three percent of breast cancer survivors may experience a cardiotoxic treatment effect. Be sure to have your weight under control and to stop smoking to decrease risk.

Nicole T. struggled with fatigue. She found that she often had to stop what she was doing and lie down. This made it difficult for her to return to her fast-paced job. She was unable to carry out the duties and responsibilities that she had prior to breast cancer. This was extremely frustrating for her, but Pilates helped her regain her energy.

12. **Impaired sensation after surgery.** This can include sensations near the incision, phantom sensations (feeling that the breast is still there after a mastectomy), or chest tightness related to tissue expanders. There have been 18 sensations reported after breast surgery, including tenderness, soreness, pulling, aches, pain, twinges, tightness, stiffness, pricking, throbbing, shooting, tingling, numbness, burning, hardness, sharpness, penetrating, and nagging. These sensations can come and go.

13. **Arthralgias** are indicated by joint pain and stiffness. One recent study found that 50% of breast cancer survivors had this condition, and 10% of those women were on Tamoxifen. You may especially notice morning stiffness in your hands or knees, as with arthritis.

14. **Weight gain.** This is probably the last thing you want to think about now. Weight gain during treatment adds insult to injury after hair loss, skin changes, and other side effects that affect your appearance. If you are overweight, using a combination of healthy diet and exercise is the best approach to get back to a healthy weight.

    Your ideal weight depends upon your height, so recommendations are based upon BMI (body mass index). It is a measure that combines height and weight. A BMI that is between 18.5 and 25 is considered healthy. The BMI Calculator app, from the National Institutes of Health, available on iOS devices, offers an easy way to determine your BMI. This information is important because weight gain may increase the risk of breast cancer recurrence. More evidence has suggested that heavier survivors are more likely to die from their cancer. Obesity also increases the risk of other health problems such as diabetes or heart disease. Having a healthy diet and participating in a regular exercise program can be a lifesaver!

    Some suggestions for getting back to a healthy weight include:

    - Eating at least 2½ cups of vegetables and fruits every day

    - Choosing 100% whole grain foods like brown rice and quinoa

    - Limiting red meat and processed meat; you can get protein from chicken, beans, or fish instead

    - Cutting down on bad fats (saturated and trans fats) and eating more polyunsaturated and monounsaturated fats such as olive oil

    - Exercise: Slowly build up to 30 minutes or more of moderate aerobic activity such as brisk walking or riding a stationary bike for five or more days a week, an equivalent of 150 minutes per week. Engage in strength training twice a week (Pilates counts!).

What muscles are affected by breast cancer surgery?

For the best rehabilitative experience, it is important for you to understand the muscles and other anatomy that have been affected by your breast cancer surgery. We will now explain which anatomical structures have been affected, where they are, what they do, and why you need to rehabilitate after surgery.

If you received a lumpectomy (Figure 1), the cancerous tissue was removed along with a margin of clean tissue. Usually, a sentinel node biopsy is performed along with this procedure, and if the node is positive (indicating cancer) then an axillary lymph node dissection (usually removal of 12–15 lymph nodes) is performed. Since tissue has been removed from the axillary area (the area directly under the joint where the arm connects to the shoulder, also known as the armpit or underarm) this can affect your ability to raise your arm up toward your head, to the side, behind your back, or behind the head as a result of scar tissue build up.

Mastectomies (Figure 2) and modified radical mastectomies (Figure 3) remove more breast tissue and modified radical mastectomies also remove lymph nodes These procedures can result in more disfigurement as well as loss of range of motion and function.

Did you know that the breast area is very large and extends from the clavicle bone to the last four ribs and from the sternum to the underarm? Breast tissue overlies the uppermost portion of the *rectus abdominis* (Figure 4) as well as the *pectoralis major* (chest muscle) (Figure 4). As a result, the *pectoralis major* can be affected by breast cancer surgeries, especially mastectomies, making shoulder and arm movement difficult to the side, to the back, behind the

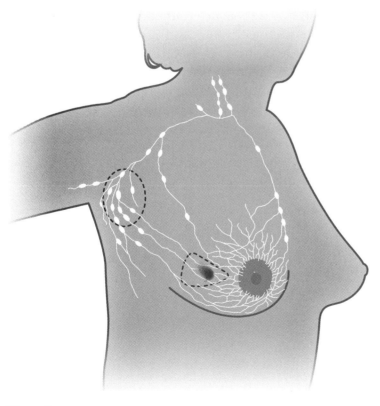

**Figure 1:
Lumpectomy.**

head, and up. This can even affect movement of our ribs during deep breathing.

Other shoulder and scapula muscles that can be tight and limited include the *serratus anterior* and *latissimus dorsi* (Figure 4). In addition, the *rectus abdominis* can be affected, especially if you received a TRAM flap reconstruction or a mastectomy.

The *pectoralis major* (Figure 4) lies right behind the breast tissue. Its job is to help move the arm up, and rotate the arm downward and toward the side. It gets stronger when you do push-ups. This muscle is usually extremely tight, especially after mastectomies, as a result of scar tissue.

The *serratus anterior* rotates the *scapula* (shoulder blade) up and forward, called protraction. Axillary lymph node dissection might affect this muscle. For example, when you reach out to hug your significant other, this muscle is being used. It might be tight and weak after surgery.

The *latissimus dorsi* (Figure 4) moves the arm behind one's back when you scratch and also toward your side. Axillary lymph node dissection can also affect this muscle. We use this muscle to push up off a chair. It can be used in breast reconstruction and pulled forward onto the breast region.

The rectus abdominis bends the trunk forward, for example when you bend to put your socks and shoes on. This is the area that everyone is always trying to strengthen to get a "six pack" appearance. It also inserts at the ribs and is involved with Pilates breathing. The rectus abdominis is used along with fat to form a breast after a mastectomy for a

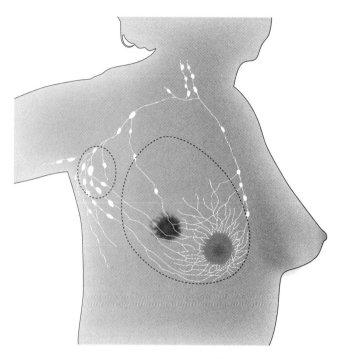

**Figure 2:
Simple Mastectomy.**

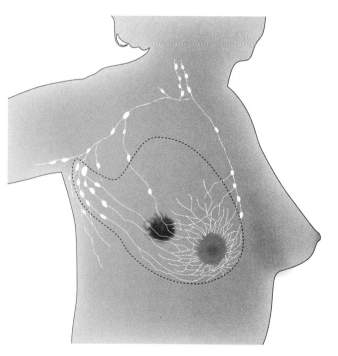

**Figure 3:
Modified Radical
Mastectomy.**

TRAM flap reconstruction. Using this muscle, can affect the strength of your core and may lead to back problems later on.

The good news is that Pilates can help rehabilitate all of these muscles.

How does Pilates help?

Pilates promotes shoulder mobility by working the scapula muscles and emphasizes good scapula stabilization. Many of the exercises, such as Scissors, Mermaid, Cane Raises, Scapula Elevation and Depression, and Scapula Protraction and Retraction, will stretch and strengthen each of the muscles mentioned above.

In addition, you will engage your Pilates "powerhouse," or core, which consists of four muscles. These are the *transverse abdominis, multifidus, pelvic floor,* and *diaphragm.*

The *transverse abdominis* (Figure 5) acts like a corset around the trunk to draw in the abdominal muscles. It is the deepest layer of abdominals. When it contracts, it acts with the *multifidus* muscle (Figure 5) in the back to stabilize the trunk. The multifidi are small muscles on either side of the spine. The function of the *pelvic floor* (Figure 5) is to hold the contents of the abdomen against gravity, including the flow of urine and feces. The pelvic floor works in conjunction with the diaphragm. Interestingly, when you activate the *transverse abdominis* for all your Pilates exercises, your pelvic floor is engaged. It can be difficult to feel when these muscles are being used. Next time when you urinate, try to stop the flow of urine. When you do this, you activate the pelvic floor. When you use the *adductor* muscles (muscles in the inner thigh) to squeeze a ball between the knees, you can help to wake up these muscles. As we get older, with certain medical conditions, or after pregnancy, the pelvic floor tends to lose strength and endurance, causing bladder control problems.

Finally, the *diaphragm* (Figure 5) is the primary muscle of respiration. It too works in conjunction with your *transverse abdominis*. Pilates breathing is sometimes called rib cage breathing, as the rib cage and chest expands three dimensionally (to the front, sides, and back) stretching the tight *pectoralis major*. Pilates breathing helps to facilitate movement, improves your lung capacity, and focuses the mind.

These four muscles all connect to the spine and foster spinal stability. Learning to activate your core will help to stabilize your spine when lifting, walking, running, or jumping. It will also help prevent abdominal weakness after TRAM flap breast reconstruction surgery, which can lead to

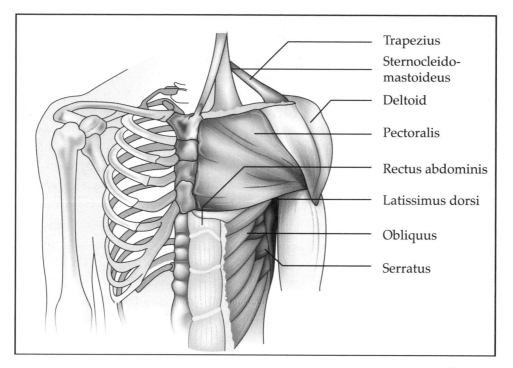

Trapezius

Sternocleido-
mastoideus

Deltoid

Pectoralis

Rectus abdominis

Latissimus dorsi

Obliquus

Serratus

Figure 4

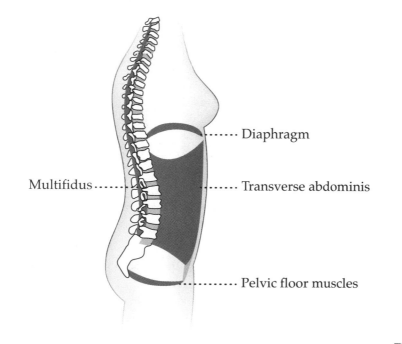

Diaphragm

Multifidus

Transverse abdominis

Pelvic floor muscles

Figure 5

back problems and impair your ability to move your trunk forward, such as when bending to tie your shoelaces.

Working these four muscles will also help to improve your posture. Good posture allows you to start from a position of strength. After breast cancer surgery, you may tend to position the affected arm (or arms) next to your side like a broken wing. Your back may round from the tightness and pain in the breast and axillary region where lymph nodes were removed. Opening up the chest and straightening the back through Pilates is important to restore breath, flexibility, and back and shoulder flexibility. In addition, proper posture can help you avoid other problems down the road. For example, a slouched posture puts a lot of pressure on the discs of the lower back. Imagine what is happening to your body after eight hours of working while seated in this posture!

Pilates teaches you to develop and use core strength rather than using more superficial muscles. This allows the shoulders to relax, the neck and head to move more easily, and relieves stress on the hips, legs, and feet. It takes stress off of the compressed organs and improves circulation.

How to Use This Book

This book includes stretches to help you get warmed up for Pilates and four different Pilates programs. Each program is divided into three phases. Phase 1 exercises will help improve your range of motion. Phases 2 and 3 are designed to improve your strength and endurance. Progressing through each phase in order will help you to safely advance and meet new challenges. Listen to your body. If treatment concerns or side effects prevent you from moving beyond Phase 1 of the program you choose, that's OK. Side effects from chemotherapy can be especially debilitating, so be sure to pace yourself and rest when needed.

Part II: Stretches: These stretches focus on the shoulders and neck, which is often tight after surgery and can contribute to loss of motion in the shoulders. Take a warm shower and do these stretches at the beginning of your exercise time as well as at the end.

Part III: Mat Pilates: If you are able to transition onto a mat, then this program is for you. Lying down on a mat in supine will help you relax and feel your muscles against the floor.

Part IV: TRAM or DIEP Flap Program: If you've had breast cancer reconstruction surgery using the abdominals, this progressive program is designed for you.

Part V: Chair Pilates: If you cannot get down on a mat yet or are unsteady on your feet, begin with this program.

Part IV: Standing Pilates: A more challenging program for those who would like to increase weight-bearing exercise and improve balance.

Pick a section that is most applicable to your situation and with which you feel most comfortable. For example, if you cannot get down to the floor or have difficulty flexing your trunk, then chair Pilates will work for you. If you would like to build and maintain healthy bones through weight-bearing exercise (any activity you do while on your feet and legs that works your muscles and bones against gravity) and do not have peripheral neuropathy or numbness in your feet, then standing Pilates is an excellent option.

Remember to be kind to yourself and listen to your body. *Start gradually* and remember that pain is a sign that you are working too hard.

On a scale from one to ten, you should feel that you are working between a three and five, with one being very mild discomfort and ten being pain such as when giving childbirth. You might feel some mild discomfort, but you should not feel pain. Breathing deeply with the Pilates breathing will help you move through more difficult movements. You should feel a mild stretch, but always work in a "pain free" zone. In the beginning, you might only be able to do three to four exercises, and that's OK. This book is not intended to overwhelm you but to provide choices! Gradually increase the number of exercises as your strength and endurance returns.

Do the exercises every day or as often as you are able each week. The more consistent and frequent you are with your exercise, the better you will feel.

Getting started

- Establish a quiet place for your practice. However, music or other calming audio, such as from an app, can be used if it soothes you.

- Make sure you have enough room to place a bath towel or a yoga or Pilates mat down on the floor to cushion the spine and lower back.

- Wear loose, comfortable clothes so you can move freely.

- Mat Pilates is usually performed barefoot, without shoes or socks. However, hard soled shoes may be worn when performing chair or standing Pilates.

You do not need to buy a lot of expensive equipment to do Pilates. Some props you can easily find around your home, such as a towels, pillows, dowels, or poles. Before buying weights, start with soup cans or filled plastic water bottles from the pantry. As your strength returns, you may find the following props useful:

- Pilates mat or bath towel. Note: a Pilates mat is thicker than a yoga mat.

- Pad, small pillow, towel, block, or other bolster to place under your head to position the neck correctly, under hips when lying prone, or to protect the breast area after reconstruction.

- Bed pillow to be placed behind back if needed during chair Pilates.

- Resistance band

- Hand weights (1–2 pounds)

- Weighted balls

Always consult with your physician or health care provider before beginning an exercise program. Stop exercise and contact your doctor if you have any of the following symptoms both during or after exercise, especially when undergoing chemotherapy:

- disorientation
- dizziness
- blurred vision or fainting
- a sudden onset of nausea or vomiting
- unusual or sudden shortness of breath

- irregular heart beat
- palpitations or chest pain
- leg/calf pain
- muscle cramps
- sudden onset of muscular weakness or fatigue

- Magic Circle

- Dowel or pole (an umbrella can be used as an alternative)

- Medium-sized playground ball (7–9" in diameter)

- Large-sized therapy ball (size depends on your height; 55–65 cm in diameter is appropriate for people 5'1"–5'8" tall)

Additional tips

1. Stretch before and after Pilates or take a warm shower to warm up the body.

2. Review the Pilates principles so that you understand what is important to do in each exercise.

3. Read the directions for each exercise carefully, note any props that may be required, and perform the modifications if needed.

4. Concentrate on a few exercises at a time and try to master those before moving on to more difficult exercises.

5. If an exercise is too difficult or painful, please ask a rehabilitation therapist or Pilates instructor for help, decrease the repetitions, lower the affected arm, or eliminate the exercise. You may experience a gentle pulling the first few weeks before the incisions have healed. Always breathe deeply while performing the exercises, and do not rush through them.

6. Do a few exercises two to three times each day to build up your strength and endurance.

7. Always alternate the exercises that focus on the arms with exercises that emphasize the legs to prevent arm fatigue, and rest when needed.

8. Once your range of motion goals have been achieved and you feel comfortable performing the Phase 1 exercises, try the Phase 2 and then the Phase 3 exercises to get stronger. If you are at risk for lymphedema (lymph node removal and/or radiation treatment), you should wear a sleeve and a gauntlet (glove) when performing resistance exercises using weights and/or bands, especially during Phase 2 or Phase 3.

9. Always remember to breathe by inhaling through the nose and exhaling through the mouth.

10. Drink plenty of water to stay hydrated.

11. It usually takes at least four weeks to establish a habit. Be patient, and keep doing your exercises.

The Pilates Principles

These principles guide each Pilates exercise to ensure that they are done correctly and safely. In Pilates, less is more. The emphasis is on a correct starting position with proper execution of the exercises. There is no wasted movement in Pilates. No more than five to eight repetitions are completed (except for the Hundreds). Breathing during each exercise is very important.

Concentrate on the correct movement patterns first and then add Pilates breathing.

If you've never done Pilates before, this may sound like a lot to think about. If possible, we recommend working with someone who is trained in Pilates first to get you on the right track.

1) Breathing

Breathing oxygenates the blood and connects the mind and body. It is the link between the sympathetic "fight or flight" and the parasympathetic "calming" nervous system. Breathing during Pilates will enhance your relaxation, improve your focus, and help to activate your muscles. Each breath is used to initiate and support movement in Pilates. You'll want to connect your breath to every Pilates movement. For the purpose of this book, this means inhaling to prepare for the exercise and then exhaling with each movement. However, this can vary from one exercise to another.

Pilates breathing is called "rib cage breathing" or costal breathing because the rib cage expands as you inhale and knits together as you exhale.

Inhale through the nose as if to smell the roses. Place your fingers on your rib cage and feel your rib cage expand.

Exhale through pursed lips as if to blow out candles, drawing the belly in toward your spine. This activates the transverse abdominis muscle. The deeper the exhalation, the more this muscle is activated. Activation of this muscle should feel very gentle, as it is more like a subtle tightening of the abdomen. The lower back and pelvis should remain still. Buttocks and thighs should stay relaxed.

Coordinating the breath with the movement is the goal. This may be difficult at first, but please stay with it. If you get confused, don't hold your breath—keep breathing!

> Using the rib cage breathing and working my abdominals elongated my rib cage, allowing for scar tissue management.
>
> —*Beth Mast*

2) Concentration

You must place intentional focus on every movement. You will feel each exercise more if you close your eyes once you become more familiar with the movements. After surgery, you may lose the ability to feel if your muscles are working properly. Closing your eyes will help in this process, allowing you to listen to your body and refocus your mind upon proper body movement.

3) Control

To be in control means that you maintain the proper form, alignment, and effort during the exercise. You don't want to throw your body around. If there is jerkiness, shaking, tightness, and/or pain you are not in control. You can limit the movement and make it smaller if necessary to regain control.

4) Centering

In Pilates, all movements come from the "powerhouse," or core. These are the abdominal muscles that we described earlier. Learning to use the powerhouse correctly will improve your posture, stabilize the spine, and improve your quality of movement. Thus, every exercise is an abdominal exercise. Each exercise incorporates the diaphragm, transverse abdominis, pelvic floor, and multifidus. Visualizing a corset around the waist will help you to activate these muscles.

5) Precision

Every exercise should be performed with precision and an emphasis upon proper form. Proper starting position and posture is crucial, as is performing the exercises slowly and without momentum.

6) Balanced Muscle Development

Everything that is done on one side of the body must also be done on the other side. For example, if you do an exercise with your right arm, you must also do it with your left.

7) Rhythm/Flow

All movements in Pilates are done with a sense of rhythm. The movements should be graceful and smooth.

8) Whole Body Movement

The whole body is engaged through breathing, engagement of the core, and use of the arms and legs (even though some exercises will not use the arms at all).

9) Relaxation

Breathing assists with the relaxation of muscles throughout the body. Unwanted tension should be released prior to beginning the exercises. You may work one body part and relax the others.

Advisories

If you are undergoing a breast implant expander program, please adhere to your physician's guidelines for movement, only raise your arms to a point where they are in line with your shoulders (90°), and do not use weights or resistance bands until you have received your doctor's clearance.

Anemia (low red blood cell count)
Anemia may affect your endurance. You may need to scale back your exercise.

Lower back issues or conditions such as spondylolisthesis, spinal stenosis and spinal arthritis

For these back issues as well as some disc injuries and sacroiliac joint dysfunctions, please consult with your health care provider before proceeding. Neutral spine may not be appropriate for you. Per your provider's approval, an imprinted spine would be used instead for all exercises.

Lymphedema

If you have lymphedema, or are at risk, it is wise to work in conjunction with a lymphedema therapist to make sure that you are not progressing too aggressively. It may be recommended that you wear a sleeve and a gauntlet when exercising. Upper body movement should be limited to a few repetitions with little or no weight. Begin the exercises without weights so that you understand how to do them correctly. Some exercises such as Mermaid, Alternate Arm and Leg Lift, Cat Stretch, or Swan may be too rigorous for you at first because they place a lot of body weight on the upper extremities. The affected arm (which may be the nonworking arm) should be lowered to a position of comfort when performing side lying exercises. If side lying exercises are not comfortable, they should be eliminated. Weights and repetitions should not be increased at the same time, and exercises that incorporate just the upper body should be alternated with those that focus on the lower body.

Metastatic Cancer

If your cancer has metastasized to the hip or spine, many of the osteoporosis recommendations apply here. It is highly recommended that you perform the chair Pilates routine.

Neutropenia (low white blood cell count)

Neutropenia may affect your ability to fight infection, so if you have a fever above 100.4° F, exercise should be avoided.

Osteoporosis

Many survivors are at risk of osteoporosis as a result of premature menopause attributable to chemotherapy and aromatase inhibitors. Be sure that you have a baseline DEXA to determine your bone density and where you may have low bone density.

Osteoporosis in the spine is a contraindication (potential danger) in many of the Pilates exercises, given their emphasis upon spinal movement and bending of the spine forward. The chair program would be a good option for women with osteoporosis, and the standing Pilates program could be a good option as well, provided that you follow the instructions for safety.

If you have low bone density in the spine, do not lift your head off the floor when lying supine, turn your spine to the right or left or bend sideways to the right or left. Modify the exercises by keeping your head on the mat. You can still get a good core workout.

If you have osteoporosis in the hip, much of the side leg series should be modified with smaller movements or eliminated from your program.

Peripheral neuropathy

Peripheral neuropathy can cause numbness as well as weakness in the hands and feet. Be sure to check your feet daily since sensation in that area may have lessened. Use care while moving since Pilates is usually conducted with bare feet. You may want to wear shoes with nonslip soles for extra grip and traction to decrease your risk of falling when moving. Seated Pilates may be a good option for you. Standing Pilates may not be safe due to the possibility of impaired balance.

Thrombocytopenia (low platelet count)

Thrombocytopenia can result in increased risk of bruising and bleeding. Activities with a high risk of injury or falling should be avoided. The chair program would be an excellent option if you have this complication.

Wrist or hand injuries

Wrist or hand injuries may require modifications such as eliminating hand weights and bearing weight on your forearms instead of your wrists (Swan) or eliminating exercises that place maximum weight on the hands, such as Alternate Arm and Leg Lift or Cat Stretch. Fitness gloves, such as WAGs (Wrist Assured Gloves; www.wristassuredgloves.com) may help you.

Stretches

Stretching helps to promote flexibility or range of motion in the joints. The stretches provided here will help to release tension in the neck, shoulders, and back in preparation for movement. You can do these stretches once you have gotten the green light from your physician. March in place for three to five minutes or take a warm shower to warm up first. Do these stretches before and after your Pilates exercises. When you feel tension in the incisional area, try to breathe through it but do not go to the point of pain when beginning this program.

Begin by holding each stretch for 10 to 20 seconds and then increase by 20 to 30 seconds at a time. If you can only hold for a few seconds at first that is perfectly OK. Do five to ten repetitions.

Neck Stretches: No Stretch

Goal: Stretching the neck muscles promotes neck mobility and shoulder flexibility. The No Stretch facilitates easier neck movements such as when driving or crossing the street.

Contraindications: Check with your physician if there are any known neck issues.

Equipment: None.

▶ **Start:**

Stand or sit with feet hip distance apart, gaze forward, and neck straight. There should be a space between your chin and chest as if holding an orange between them.

▶ **Stretch:**

Inhale and then exhale as you rotate your head to the right looking over your right shoulder.
Hold for 10 to 20 seconds, breathing regularly.
Inhale and return to center.
Repeat to the left side, and look over your left shoulder as you hold for 10 to 20 seconds, breathing regularly. This should look as if you were saying "No" very slowly.

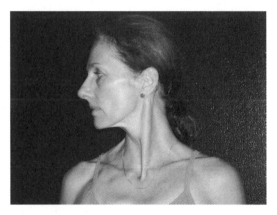

▶ **Be sure to:**

Keep both shoulders relaxed and be sure not to lift them up as you turn.

Neck Stretches: Yes Stretch

Goal: To increase neck mobility, making looking up into a closet or down at your feet easier.

Contraindications: Check with your physician if there are any known neck issues.

Equipment: None.

▶ Start:

Stand or sit with feet hip distance apart, gaze forward, and neck straight. There should be a space between your chin and chest as if holding an orange between them.

▶ Stretch:

Inhale, then exhale and raise your chin up toward the ceiling and hold for 10 seconds, breathing regularly.

Inhale, then bring your chin down toward the floor as you exhale and hold for 10 seconds, breathing regularly.

Think of this exercise as if you are saying "Yes" very slowly.

▶ Be sure to:

Hold shoulders down when moving the neck.

Neck Stretches: Ears to Shoulders

Goal: To stretch the area between your neck and shoulder.

Contraindications: Check with your physician if there are any known neck issues.

Equipment: None.

▶ **Start:**

Stand or sit with feet hip distance apart. Gaze forward, with your neck straight and a space between your chin and chest.

▶ **Stretch:**

Inhale, then exhale as you bring your right ear to your right shoulder. Hold for 10 to 20 seconds, breathing regularly.

Inhale as you return neck to center.

Exhale, then bring the left ear to the left shoulder and hold for 10 to 20 seconds, breathing regularly.

Inhale as you return neck to center.

▶ **Modification:**

For an added stretch, take your right hand and gently draw the right side of your head to the right shoulder. Then do the same on the left side.

▶ **Be sure to:**

Only stretch within a pain-free zone and pull gently.

Standing Wall Angels

Goal: To open up the pectoralis major and minor chest muscles and improve shoulder mobility. To fly like a bird, these muscles must be loose. This stretch may take time to master, so be patient.

Contraindications: If you have had a mastectomy, transverse rectus abdominis myocutaneous (TRAM) or deep inferior epigastric perforator (DIEP) flap reconstruction, or are undergoing a breast implant expander program, this exercise may be too strenuous at first; eliminate it.

Equipment: Wall.

▶ Start:

Stand with back leaning against wall, feet 6 to 12 inches away from wall and hip distance apart, in parallel.

Arms are raised in the "goalpost" position against the wall. Gaze forward, neck straight, with a space between your chin and chest.

▶ **Stretch:**

Inhale, then exhale as you slide your arms up along the wall until they are almost straight.

Hold for 10 to 20 seconds at the highest point within your comfort zone, breathing regularly.

Inhale as you return to the start position.

▶ **Be sure to:**

Keep both shoulder blades on the wall equally and do not lift up your shoulders toward your ears.

 This exercise really helped to stretch my arms and chest.

—*Grace T.*

Seated Chest Opener

Goal: To stretch the chest and shoulder muscles, strengthen the middle back muscles, and improve posture.

Contraindications: If you are undergoing a breast expander program or have undergone TRAM or DIEP flap reconstruction, see the modification.

Equipment: Chair.

Medium-sized ball (optional; squeezing the ball between your knees will help to activate the pelvic floor and transverse abdominis muscles).

▶ Start:

Sit on the edge of a chair.

Place hands gently behind the ears but do not interlace them.

▶ Stretch:

Inhale, then exhale as you bring elbows out to the side like wings. Imagine cracking a walnut between your shoulder blades. The movement may be small.

Hold for 10 to 20 seconds as you inhale and exhale. You will feel the muscles in your middle back working.

Inhale as you return elbows to start position.

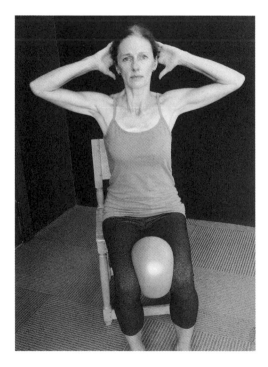
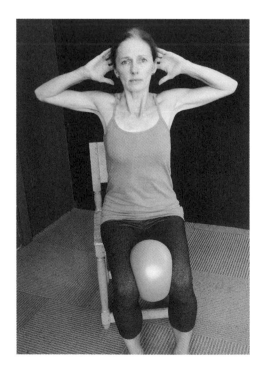

▶ **Be sure to:**

Work within a pain-free zone.

▶ **Modification:**

Place hands on chest with elbows at your sides rather than behind the ears. Bring your elbows out to your sides like wings and hold. Then, bring them down slowly to the start positions as if flapping your wings. The movement may be small.

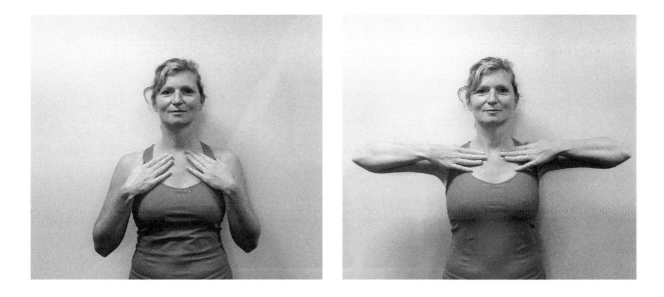

Interlace Hands in Front and Over Head

Goal: To stretch your wrists, forearms, shoulders, and upper back.

Contraindications: If you are undergoing a breast implant expander program or have undergone TRAM or DIEP flap reconstruction, do not move your arms past 90 degrees until cleared by your doctor.

Equipment: Medium-sized ball (optional if performing this exercise while seated; squeezing the ball between your knees will help to activate the pelvic floor and transverse abdominis muscles).

▶ Start:

This stretch can be done sitting or standing.

Sitting: Sit on the edge of a chair.

Standing: Stand with feet hip distance apart.

Gaze forward, with your neck straight and a space between your chin and chest.

Extend both arms in front of you and interlace them together. Palms will be facing toward you.

▶ Stretch:

Inhale, then exhale as you lift both arms up toward your head.

Inhale, then exhale as you hold for 10 to 20 seconds, breathing regularly.

Inhale, then exhale as you return to the start position.

Inhale, then exhale as you turn hands so palms face away from you.

Inhale, and then exhale as you hold for 10 to 20 seconds, breathing regularly.

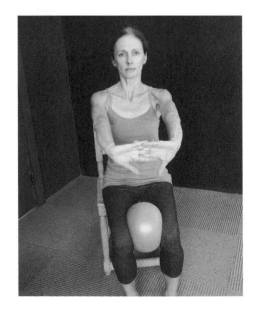

▶ **Be sure to:**

Keep your shoulders down; do not lift them up. Be careful not to move your head forward as you lift your arms overhead.

▶ **Modification: To lessen the intensity:**

- Bend elbows to decrease the stretch in wrists and shoulders.

Towel Stretches: Side Body Stretch

Goal: Use of a towel can help you to stretch; use either a face or bath towel. This stretch addresses the sides of your body including the latissimus dorsi as well as the axillary area under your arms where lymph nodes may have been removed. These muscles are important when reaching to get something off of a shelf.

Contraindications: This exercise is not recommended if you have osteoporosis in the spine. If you are undergoing a breast implant expander program or have undergone TRAM or DIEP flap reconstruction, this exercise is not recommended until you have received clearance.

Equipment: Face or bath towel.
Medium-sized ball (optional if performing this exercise while seated; squeezing the ball between your knees will help to activate the pelvic floor and transverse abdominis muscles).

▶ **Start:**
This stretch can be done sitting or standing.
Sitting: Sit at the edge of a chair without arms.
Standing: Stand with feet hip distance apart.
Gaze forward, with your neck straight and a space between your chin and chest.
Hold a towel horizontally with both hands, shoulder width apart.

▶ Stretch:

Inhale, then exhale as you bring the towel up overhead.

Inhale, then exhale as you raise both arms up and over to the right. You will be making a diagonal line with your towel. You will feel a stretch on the left side of your body. Hold for 10 to 20 seconds, breathing regularly.

Inhale as you return to center, and exhale to repeat on the left side. You will feel a stretch down the right side of your body.

▶ Be sure to:

Keep both shoulder blades down and work within a pain-free zone.

Towel Stretches: "W" Stretch

Goal: To improve your posture by stretching the tight pectoralis muscles and strengthening the middle trapezius.

Contraindications: If you are undergoing a breast implant expander program or have undergone TRAM or DIEP flap reconstruction, this exercise is not recommended until you have received clearance.

Equipment: A face or bath towel.
Medium-sized ball (optional if performing this exercise while seated; squeezing the ball between your knees will help to activate the pelvic floor and transverse abdominis muscles).

▶ **Start:**
This stretch can be done sitting or standing.
Sitting: Sit at the edge of a chair with feet hip distance apart.
Standing: Stand with feet hip distance apart.
Gaze forward, with your neck straight and a space between your chin and chest.
Hold a towel horizontally at each end with both hands shoulder width apart.

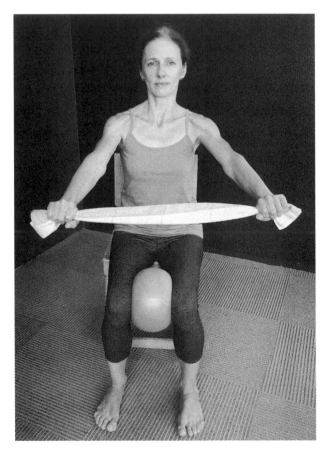

▶ Stretch:

Inhale and then exhale as you bend elbows back to form the letter "W." Hold for 10 to 20 seconds, breathing regularly. You will feel your back muscles working.

Inhale and return to start position.

▶ Be sure to:

Only perform to the point of mild discomfort, not pain. This exercise is challenging.

PART III

Mat Pilates Program

If cleared by your physician, you may begin mat Pilates with drains in place. Proceed carefully until drains are removed, approximately 10 to 14 days after surgery. If you do not have drains or had a lumpectomy without lymph node dissection, you may be able to begin these exercises on day one after surgery. If you find it difficult to get down onto the floor, these exercises can be done in bed.

For two weeks following your doctors' clearance to exercise, it is important to only do what you can within your pain and fatigue level and your tolerance. It is better to perform fewer repetitions if necessary, or eliminate exercises, than to push yourself beyond what you are capable of. Working with an occupational therapist or physical therapist who is educated in the special needs and concerns of the breast cancer survivor can be a good starting point.

If you are at risk for lymphedema, wear a sleeve and gauntlet (glove) if recommended by your health care professional. Progress slowly when using weights and do not increase the number of repetitions at the same time that you increase the weights. Start with light weights such as 1 pound.

If you are undergoing a breast implant expander program, or have undergone a Transverse Rectus Abdominis Myocutaneous (TRAM), or Deep Inferior Epigastric Perforator (DIEP) flap reconstruction, do not use weights or resistance bands until cleared by your doctor, and eliminate or modify exercises as indicated.

If you have back issues, always use an imprinted spine, not a neutral spine, for all exercises.

If you have osteoporosis or osteopenia in the spine, avoid flexing or turning your back.

If you are undergoing chemotherapy, adhere to your physician's recommendations and precautions.

Phase 1: Protective Phase

Do three to five repetitions of each of these exercises, on each side of the body. This phase will last approximately two weeks, or until you feel comfortable progressing to more difficult exercises. The exercises should feel easier and there should be no discomfort before moving on to the next phase. The exercises should be done in this order to establish a daily routine.

The goal of this phase is to ensure tissue healing without sacrificing range of motion and flexibility of the chest and arm. In these exercises, only move your arms until they align with your shoulders at a 90° angle, and during this phase try to use your affected arm normally to perform daily living tasks such as brushing your teeth, putting on deodorant, or wiping up your kitchen table.

When you move on to Phase 2 and Phase 3, use the exercises in Phase 1 as your warm-up.

- Pelvic Tilts: Neutral and Imprinted Spine
- Breathing
- Supine Neck Releases
- Scapula Elevation and Depression
- Scapula Protraction and Retraction
- Elbow Flexion and Extension
- Bridging
- Heel Slides
- Marching
- Cane Raises

Phase 2: Return to Function

Once you are comfortable with the Phase 1 exercises and medically cleared, add the exercises in Phase 2 to your routine for at least two weeks. Alternate arm and leg exercises to decrease fatigue. Begin with three to five repetitions of each exercise, gradually increasing to five to eight. Work within your comfort zone.

- Arm Scissors
- Floating Arms
- Toe Taps
- Hundred, Feet Down
- Side Lying Chest Opener, Part 1
- Back Stretch

After two weeks with these exercises, or when you are comfortable, add the following:

- Leg Circles
- Single Leg Kick
- Baby Swan
- Mermaid

Phase 3: Regaining Strength, Power, and Endurance

Once you are able to do the exercises in Phases 1 and 2 without pain or discomfort, add the following to your routine. Begin with three to five repetitions of each exercise, gradually increasing to five to eight.

- Side Lying Rotator Cuff Push

- Side Lying Chest Opener, Part 2

- Double Leg Kick

- Swimming

- Side Lying Leg Series

- Hundred

- Criss Cross, Feet Down

For all exercises, five to eight repetitions maximum is recommended. However, everyone is different and you should work within your own tolerance. Treatment side effects can interfere with your strength and endurance. How you feel can vary from day to day, so please be gentle with yourself.

Please remember:

- Stretch before and after Pilates or take a warm shower to warm up the body.

- A pad, small pillow, towel, or block under your head can help place your head in the proper position when side lying or supine.

- A medium-sized ball between your knees will help you to activate the pelvic floor and transverse abdominis muscles so that you can feel the muscles working. You will feel a flutter in the abdominal region when the transverse abdominis muscle is activated. However, sensation may be impaired after surgery in the abdominal region as well as the chest.

- Always alternate arm and leg exercises to prevent fatigue, and rest when needed.

- Drink plenty of water to stay hydrated.

What Is Good Posture in Supine (Lying on Your Back)?

Before starting mat Pilates, do a body scan to ensure that you are starting correctly.

Questions to ask yourself:

- Are my feet aligned with my knees, with weight equally on toes as well as heels? Are my toes forward?

- Is the center of my kneecap aligned with my middle toe? Is there equal weight on both feet?

- Are my knees aligned with my hips? (Draw an imaginary line from your hips to your knees.)

- Is my pelvis level with the floor, in neutral, or is my spine imprinted if I have back issues?

- Are both hip bones pointing toward the ceiling?

- Are my arms resting at my side?

- Are my shoulders level and neutral, not lifted up to my ears?

- Are my shoulder blades in neutral (placed on the mat) so they are not pushed forward?

- Is my rib cage soft and down?

- Is my chin in and my neck long?

- Are my head and neck aligned with my spine or is my neck arched or my head too far forward? (If you are out of alignment or your neck hurts when lying on your back, use a pad, small pillow, towel, or block under your head to achieve the proper position.)

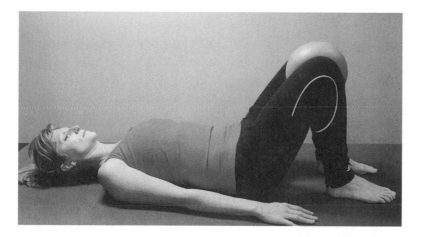

Phase 1
Protective Phase

Pelvic Tilts: Neutral and Imprinted Spine

Goal: To learn how to find a neutral pelvis, neutral spine, and an imprinted spine.

Neutral spine is the natural position of the spine when all three curves of the spine—cervical (neck), thoracic (middle), and lumbar (lower)—are present and in good alignment. This is the strongest position of the spine and supports all movement, reducing the risk of injury. This is the ideal position of the spine in most Pilates exercises, as you'll see in the instructions, but it is a goal to achieve for most of us. If you are unable to achieve neutral spine, imprint your spine.

An imprinted spine is the lower back flat against the floor, with no gaps. Imagine sinking your lower back into sand, tilting your pelvis toward your nose. Imprinting helps to protect the back in Pilates exercises that require both legs to be raised off the floor and in any exercise if you have back problems. The position of your pelvis determines the position of your spine.

Contraindications: If you have any back problems, always use an imprinted spine for all exercises.

Equipment: Pad, small pillow, towel, or block under head, if needed.
Medium-sized ball (optional; squeezing the ball between your knees will help to activate the pelvic floor and transverse abdominis muscles and prevent your knees from collapsing in).

▶ Start:

Lie on your back with both knees bent and feet on the ground, hip distance apart.
Place the ring and little fingers of both hands on your hip bones, and make a heart with your index fingers pointed toward the pubic bone. Your thumbs are pointed toward the belly button.

▶ Exercise:

Gently tilt your pelvis forward and backward several times until both hands are on the same plane and parallel to the floor. This is your neutral pelvis. When your pelvis is in neutral, your spine is in neutral.

- Neutral = Thumbs and index fingers should be on the same plane and is halfway between the two positions.

From neutral, gently tilt your pelvis to your nose so your back is flat against the floor. Your thumbs will be lower than your index fingers. Now your spine is imprinted.

(*continued*)

- Imprinted = Gently tilt pelvis to nose. Your thumbs will be lower than your index fingers. This is used to support the lower back during exercises where the legs are raised off the floor, or with certain back conditions. Think *lower back to the floor using your abdominal muscles.* Do not squeeze your buttocks or thighs. They should stay relaxed.

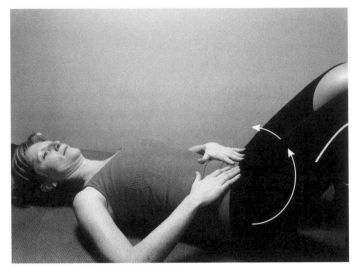

Note: Model is in neutral. To imprint, follow the arrows.

Breathing

Goal: To learn the Pilates breathing method of rib cage breathing, relax the chest area, and prepare the body for exercise. This breathing helps in stretching the tight pectoralis major muscle after surgery as well as in learning how to activate the transverse abdominis. Always do this when experiencing discomfort in your chest or axillary areas.

Contraindications: None.

Equipment: Pad, small pillow, towel, or block under head, if needed.
Medium-sized ball (optional; squeezing the ball between your knees will help to activate the pelvic floor and transverse abdominis muscles).

▶ Start:

Lie on your back with both knees bent and feet on the floor, hip distance apart.
Pelvis is level with the floor, in neutral, or imprinted if you have back problems.
Hands on rib cage.

▶ Exercise:

Inhale to "smell the roses" and feel your rib cage expand to the front, sides, and back. This is called rib cage breathing.
Exhale "to blow out the candles" as you feel your rib cage grow smaller. This will help to activate the correct muscles and promote relaxation.

▶ Be sure to:

Rise from the floor slowly. Many of us are not used to breathing deeply so you may feel a bit dizzy after performing deep breathing.

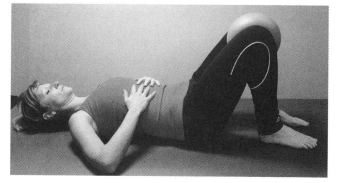

Supine Neck Releases

Goal: To release tight neck muscles such as the sternocleidomastoid and improve shoulder flexibility.

Contraindications: If you have any neck issues that cause pain, eliminate this exercise.

Equipment: Pad, small pillow, towel, or block under head, if needed.

Medium-sized ball (optional; squeezing the ball between your knees will help to activate the pelvic floor and transverse abdominis muscles).

▶ **Start:**

Lie on your back with both knees bent and feet on the ground, hip distance apart.

Pelvis is level with the floor, in neutral, or imprinted if you have back problems.

Both arms are resting by your sides and your eyes are looking up toward the ceiling.

Arms are long at your sides.

▶ **Exercise:**

Inhale to start, then exhale as you rotate your head to the right. Hold the stretch for 10 to 20 seconds, breathing regularly.

Inhale and return head to center.

Exhale to repeat the same sequence on the left side.

▶ **Be sure to:**

Keep both shoulders on the ground and shoulder blades down as you turn your neck.

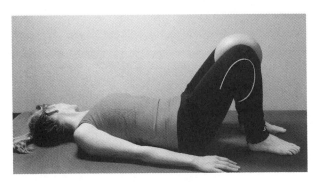

Scapula Elevation and Depression

Goal: To warm up the scapular muscles, including the upper and middle trapezius, and prepare for shoulder exercises.

Contraindications: None.

Equipment: Pad, small pillow, towel, or block under head, if needed.
Medium-sized ball (optional; squeezing the ball between your knees will help to activate the pelvic floor and transverse abdominis muscles and prevent your knees from collapsing in).

▶ Start:

Lie on your back with both knees bent and feet on the ground, hip distance apart.

Pelvis is level with the floor, in neutral, or imprinted if you have back problems.

Your arms are long by your sides, reaching for the opposite wall.

This exercise also can be done either in a sitting or standing position with arms long at your sides.

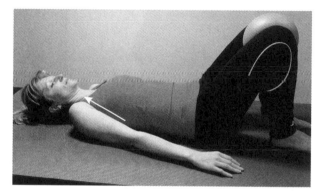

Elevation

▶ Exercise:

Inhale as you slide your shoulder blades (back wing bones) up toward your ears (elevation). Exhale as you slide your shoulder blades down (depression). Imagine your shoulder blades are sliding gently into your back pockets.

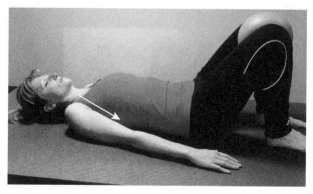

Depression

▶ Be sure to:

Keep both shoulders on the mat as you slide your shoulders up and down. Don't allow your shoulders to round forward.

Scapula Protraction and Retraction

Goal: To warm up the shoulders in preparation for movement, as well as strengthen the scapular muscles, such as the serratus anterior and rhomboids, necessary for proper shoulder movement.

Contraindications: None.

Equipment: Pad, small pillow, towel, or block under head, if needed.
Medium-sized ball (optional; squeezing the ball between your knees will help to activate the pelvic floor and transverse abdominis muscles and prevent your knees from collapsing in).

▶ **Start:**

Lie on your back with both knees bent and feet on the ground, hip distance apart.

Pelvis is level with the floor, in neutral, or imprinted if you have back problems.

Arms and fingertips are reaching toward the ceiling at no more than a 90° angle to your shoulders.

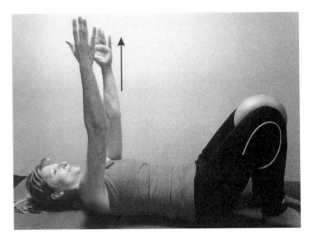

Protraction

▶ **Exercise:**

Inhale and reach fingertips toward the ceiling (shoulder blades will lift off the mat). This is protraction.

Exhale and bring your shoulder blades together (not too hard) as you imagine you are gently cracking a walnut between your shoulder blades. This is retraction.

Retraction

▶ **Modification: For an added challenge:**

- Stretch a resistance band between your hands. If you are undergoing a breast implant expander program or have undergone TRAM or DIEP flap reconstruction, do not use a resistance band until medically cleared.

"After surgery, I didn't have the same range of motion. I couldn't do normal activities like scoop ice cream for my kids or use a salad spinner. Pilates helped me work on my range of motion and now it is almost back to normal."

—*Sharon B.*

Elbow Flexion and Extension

Goal: To decrease swelling in the arms after surgery and maintain range of motion.

Contraindications: None.

Equipment: Pad, small pillow, towel, or block under head, if needed.
Medium-sized therapy ball (optional; squeezing the ball between your knees will help to activate the pelvic floor and transverse abdominis muscles).
Magic Circle, ball, towel, pole, or umbrella held between both hands.

▶ Start:

Lie on your back with both knees bent and feet on the ground, hip distance apart.

Pelvis is level with the floor, in neutral, or imprinted if you have back problems.

Hold the outside of a Magic Circle between your palms, with fingertips up and elbows slightly bent.

▶ Exercise:

Inhale, then exhale as you bend elbows toward you.

Inhale and hold this position. This is flexion.

Exhale as you extend your elbows and return to the start position. This is extension.

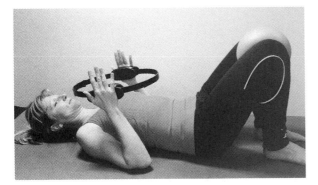

Flexion

Extension

Bridging

Goal: To warm up the spine as well as your hamstrings and gluteal muscles. This exercise will help make it easier to put on your underwear and pants and reposition yourself in bed.

Contraindications: Check with your physician to make sure that this exercise is safe for you to do when recovering with drains in place.

Equipment: Pad, small pillow, towel, or block under head, if needed.
Medium-sized ball (optional; squeezing the ball between your knees will help to activate the pelvic floor and transverse abdominis muscles and prevent your knees from collapsing in).

▶ Start:

Lie on your back with both knees bent and feet on the ground, hip distance apart.
Pelvis is level with the floor, in neutral, or imprinted if you have back problems.
Arms are long at your sides.

▶ Exercise:

Inhale to start, and then exhale as you tilt your pelvis toward your nose to imprint your spine.

Push off through your heels and lift your spine off the mat one vertebra at a time. You will start moving the lower back, middle back, and then upper back off the mat.

Inhale as you hold this position at the point where you can remain still, without any movement of your pelvis. The upper part of both your shoulder blades should remain on the mat.

Exhale as you return to the start position by gradually bringing the upper back, middle back, and lower back gently down to the mat, vertebra by vertebra, to your neutral or imprinted pelvis. Think of rolling the spine slowly down to the floor.

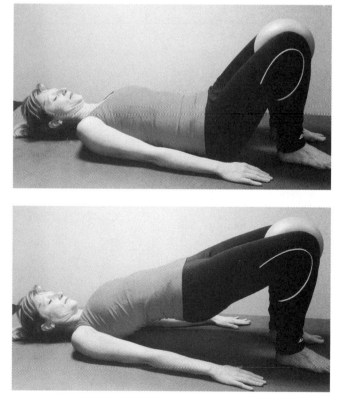

▶ Be sure to:

Keep both shoulder blades on the mat. Do not let the pelvis rock forward and backward or side to side.

(continued)

▶ **Modifications: For an added challenge:**

- Hold a Magic Circle between your inner thighs for resistance as you lift your hips.

- Hold a Magic Circle between your palms with hands facing each other and fingertips toward the ceiling. Squeeze it when the hips are lifted.

Heel Slides

Goal: To gain stability in your pelvic region, activate your transverse abdominis, and improve hamstring flexibility.

Contraindications: None.

Equipment: Pad, small pillow, towel, or block under head, if needed.
Small toning balls under the toes to help with movement (optional) or small towel under the ball of the foot to facilitate movement.

▶ Start:

Lie on your back with both knees bent and feet on the ground, hip distance apart.
Pelvis is level with the floor, in neutral, or imprinted if you have back problems.
Hands are resting on pelvis.

▶ Exercise:

Inhale to start, and then exhale to press the right heel away to extend the leg out.
Inhale to return to start position.
Perform all repetitions on one leg, and then switch. When this is mastered, alternate sides.

▶ Be sure to:

Keep the pelvis stable; do not let the pelvis rock. Both hips should be facing toward the ceiling as you extend the leg out.
Only go as far as is comfortable for you. If you have tight hamstrings, you may not be able to extend the legs all the way out.

Marching

Goal: To activate and strengthen your transverse abdominis and help make walking easier.

Contraindications: None.

Equipment: Pad, small pillow, towel, or block under head, if needed.

▶ **Start:**

Lie on your back with both knees bent and feet on the ground, hip distance apart.

Pelvis is level with the floor, in neutral, or imprinted if you have back problems.

Arms are long at your sides.

▶ **Exercise:**

Inhale to start and then exhale to lift your right foot off the floor without moving your pelvis. Imagine that your pelvis is anchored into the mat. You may only be able to lift your leg a few inches at first.

Inhale to return your foot to the floor.

Alternate legs as if marching in place.

▶ **Be sure to:**

Keep your pelvis stable. It should not rock from side to side or forward and backward. Keep both hip bones facing the ceiling. Tailbone should remain on the mat as you move your leg up.

Cane Raises

Goal: To increase range of motion and stability in the shoulder, necessary for putting on garments or reaching overhead as well as stretching the latissimus dorsi muscle, which is often tight after surgery.

Contraindications: Only move your arms to 90°, especially if you are undergoing a breast implant expander program or have undergone TRAM or DIEP flap reconstruction.
If you still have drains, only proceed within your physician's guidelines.

Equipment: Pad, small pillow, towel, or block under head, if needed.
Medium-sized ball (optional; squeezing the ball between your knees will help to activate the pelvic floor and transverse abdominis muscles and prevent your knees from collapsing in).
Cane, pole, towel, or umbrella.

▶ **Start:**

Lie on your back with both knees bent and feet on the ground, hip distance apart.
Pelvis is level with the floor, in neutral, or imprinted if you have back problems.
Arms are at hips, hands holding the cane, towel, pole, or umbrella.

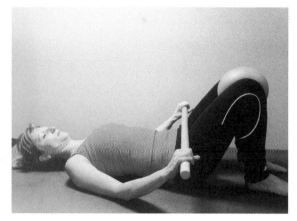

▶ **Exercise:**

Inhale to start as you imprint your shoulder blades on the mat, and then exhale to lift cane until arms are at a 90° angle to your shoulders. Inhale as you hold.
Exhale as you return your arms to the starting position.

▶ **Be sure to:**

Keep your shoulder blades on the mat. Don't let your rib cage pop out or your back arch while lifting your arms above your head. Work within your comfort zone.

Phase 2

Return to Function

Arm Scissors

Goal: To increase range of motion and stability in your shoulders, useful for washing windows, pulling down a shade, and putting on and taking off a hat.

Contraindications: If you are undergoing a breast implant expander program, omit this exercise.

Equipment: Pad, small pillow, towel, or block under head, if needed. Medium-sized ball (optional; squeezing the ball between your knees will help to activate the pelvic floor and transverse abdominis muscles and prevent your knees from collapsing in).

▶ **Start:**

Lie on your back with both knees bent and feet on the ground, hip distance apart.

Pelvis is level with the floor, in neutral, or imprinted if you have back problems.

Arms are reaching toward the ceiling at a 90° angle to shoulders with palms facing one another.

▶ **Exercise:**

Inhale to start, and then exhale to lift your right arm over your head.

Inhale to bring your right arm down to your side.

Exhale to lift your left arm over your head.

Inhale to lower your left arm to your side while raising your right arm over your head.

Continue alternating arms.

▶ **Be sure to:**

Keep your rib cage and shoulder blades down and flush against the mat. Work within your comfort zone.

(*continued*)

▷ Modification: For an added challenge:

- Add light hand weights (1–2 pounds).
  If you are undergoing a breast implant expander program or have undergone TRAM or DIEP flap reconstruction, do not use weights until cleared by your doctor.

Floating Arms

Goal: To increase range of motion and flexibility in the shoulder, making it easier to dress and put on and take off clothing such as hats and jackets.

Contraindications: If you are undergoing a breast implant expander program, only lift arms to 90° and keep arm circles low until cleared by your doctor.

Equipment: Pad, small pillow, towel, or block under head, if needed.
Medium-sized ball (optional; squeezing the ball between your knees will help to activate the pelvic floor and transverse abdominis muscles and prevent your knees from collapsing in).

▶ **Start:**

Lie on your back with both knees bent and feet on the ground, hip distance apart. Pelvis is level with the floor, in neutral, or imprinted if you have back problems. Arms are long at your sides.

▶ **Exercise:**

Inhale to start, and then exhale as you raise arms to the ceiling, palms facing in.
Inhale as you hold.

Exhale as you bring arms down to your sides in a T-position, both palms up, and then circle arms down to your sides.

(continued)

▶ **Caution:**

Keep shoulder blades on the mat, and be sure to work within your comfort zone. This exercise is challenging.

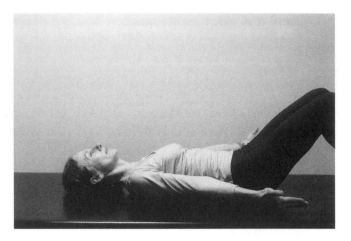

▶ **Modification: For an added challenge:**

- Add light hand weights (1–2 pounds) or weighted balls. If you are undergoing a breast implant expander program or have undergone TRAM or DIEP flap reconstruction, do not use weights until cleared by your doctor.

Toe Taps

Goal: To bring awareness and strength to the abdominals to help with walking, going up stairs, and putting on socks or pants.

Contraindications: If lifting your legs causes pain, eliminate this exercise.

Equipment: Pad, small pillow, towel, or block under head, if needed.

▶ Start:

Lie on your back, legs lifted off the floor with knees bent so that the thighs are perpendicular to the floor and the shins are parallel to the floor. This is called being in "tabletop."
Arms are long at your sides.
Pelvis is imprinted (tilt pelvis toward your nose).

▶ Exercise:

Inhale to start, and exhale as you reach the left foot toward the floor without shifting your pelvis. You may only be able to go a few inches.
Inhale to return to start position.
Perform five to eight repetitions on one leg, and then switch to the other leg.

▶ **Be sure to:**

Keep your back and shoulder blades on the mat at all times. Decrease number of repetitions if you find this exercise challenging.

"The incorporation of the pelvic floor in Pilates has helped, as I was put through premature menopause resulting in weakness of my pelvic floor and stress incontinence."

—*Beth Mast*

Hundred, Feet Down

Goal: To strengthen the scapular muscles, such as the serratus anterior and latissimus dorsi, as well as the abdominal muscles.

Contraindications: If you have osteoporosis in the spine, do this exercise with head down. Do not lift head off mat.

Equipment: Pad, small pillow, towel, or block under head, if needed.
Medium-sized ball (optional; squeezing the ball between your knees will help to activate the pelvic floor and transverse abdominis muscles and prevent your knees from collapsing in).

▶ Start:

Lie on your back with both knees bent and feet on the ground, hip distance apart.
Pelvis is level with the floor, in neutral, or imprinted if you have back problems.
Arms are long at your sides.

▶ Exercise:

Inhale as you gently nod your chin to your chest. Exhale as you lift upper body and shoulders off the floor while stretching your arms toward your feet. Look at your belly button and keep your neck relaxed.

Pump your arms from the back of your shoulders as you inhale for five beats and then exhale for five beats. That is one cycle of 10.

Repeat the cycle 10 times for a complete Hundred or do as many cycles as you are able.

▶ Be sure to:

Make the movement come from the scapular muscles, not the elbows or head. You can support your head with one hand if necessary to protect the neck.

Side Lying Chest Opener, Part 1

Goal: To help you regain shoulder stability and open up the chest, which is often tight after surgery.

Contraindications: Proper side lying position may be difficult to achieve with affected arm on bottom. Avoid this exercise if painful.
If you have lower back problems, place a pad or towel between your knees.

Equipment: Pad, small pillow towel, or block under head, to keep neck in alignment.

▶ Start:

Lie on your side, back lined up against the edge of the mat, hips stacked on top of one another.
Knees are bent in a 90° angle at a 45° angle to the body.
Palms are stacked one on top of the other.

▶ Exercise:

Inhale to start and then exhale as you float the top arm up to the ceiling as far as possible. Follow your arm with your eyes for a more pronounced stretch.
Inhale as you hold at highest point that is comfortable for you.
Exhale and return to start position.
Perform five to eight repetitions and then switch to the other side.

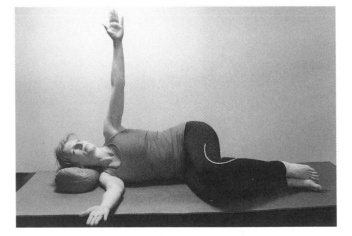

▶ **Modification: For an added challenge:**

• Add a light hand weight (1–2 pounds). If you are undergoing a breast implant expander program or have undergone TRAM or DIEP flap reconstruction, do not use weights until cleared by your doctor.

Back Stretch

Goal: To stretch the shoulders, sides of the body, back, and hips, which are often tight after surgery.

Contraindications: If you have osteoporosis or are unable to sit on your knees, see the modification.

Equipment: Towel or blanket (optional; placed under the knees and/or buttocks if you have tight hamstrings).

▶ **Start:**

On your knees with buttocks to heels.
The spine is rounded with arms in front.

▶ **Exercise:**

Inhale to start, then exhale as you move arms as far as possible forward on your mat. Inhale as you hold.

Exhale as you move arms to the right as hips move to the left.

Inhale as you hold.

Exhale as you move arms to the left and hips to the right.

▶ **Modification:**

If you have osteoporosis in the spine or are unable to sit on your knees, lie on your back and draw knees into your chest to stretch the back and hips.

Leg Circles

Goal: To help you learn to keep your shoulder blades and core stable and activated as you work your legs.

Equipment: Pad, small pillow, towel, or block under head, if needed.

▶ Start:

Lie on your back with both knees bent and feet on the ground, hip distance apart. Lift your right leg up straight to the ceiling as you keep the other knee bent and foot glued to the floor.
Pelvis is level with the floor, in neutral, or imprinted if you have back problems.
Arms are long at your sides, pressed into mat for stability.

▶ Exercise:

Inhale to start, then exhale as you make five to eight small circles (the smaller the better) inward with your right leg (toward the other leg).
Inhale, then exhale to reverse the direction to the outside (away from the other leg)
Return to start position.
Perform five to eight repetitions and then switch to the left leg.

▶ Be sure to:

Keep pelvis stable when creating circles. No rocking forward and backward or side to side.

▶ **Modifications:**

If you have tight hamstrings, bend the working leg.

For an added challenge:

• Extend the nonworking leg on the floor or place on top of a foam roller or ball.

Single Leg Kick

Goal: To improve bed mobility (moving in bed from one position to another) and strengthen the hamstrings and middle back. This is an excellent exercise for those with osteoporosis or osteopenia in the spine.

Contraindications: Avoid this exercise if you have lower back pain that is not resolved with the modification.

Equipment: None.

▶ **Start:**

Lie on belly with elbows bent under shoulders and palms flat on the mat in a triangle position. Chest is lifted, and head is in line with the spine.
Legs are glued together with the buttocks tight, and your belly squeezed toward the spine.
Pubic bone is pressing into your mat.

▶ **Exercise:**

Inhale as you bend your right knee and flex your heel two times toward your buttocks.
Exhale as you return to start position by lowering your leg.
Repeat on the left leg.

▶ **Modification:**

Cross arms and rest forehead on top of arms.

Baby Swan

Goal: To strengthen the middle and lower back, which will help to correct poor posture. It is an excellent exercise for those with osteoporosis or osteopenia in the spine.

Contraindications: If you have lower back pain, turn out your legs from the hips like a ballerina and be sure to press your pubic bone into the mat, but you might prefer the modification.

Equipment: None.

▶ Start:

Lie on belly with hands in front of your shoulders in a goalpost position.

Rest your forehead on the mat.

Legs are extended on the mat, hip distance apart.

Pubic bone is pressed into the mat.

▶ Exercise:

Inhale to start and then exhale to press down into your hands and lift your head and back off the mat. Pubic bone remains on mat while shoulder blades slide away from ears as you lift head and upper body off mat as one unit. Inhale as you hold and gaze forward.

Exhale and return to start position.

▶ Be sure to:

Avoid pain in your lower back. If you feel pain, you may have lifted your body too high. Reduce the height that you lift your back, or place a pad or pillow under your hip bones. Eliminate if pain persists.

▶ **Modification:**

Rest forehead on crossed arms and lift the back as one unit from this position.

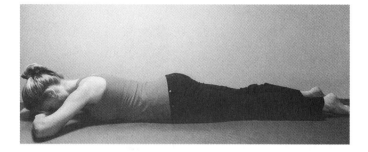

Mermaid

Goal: To help you regain the motion for reaching toward an item across your chest or above your head, such as when playing ball with your child, playing tennis, or reaching for an item on a shelf. This exercise also helps stretch the latissimus dorsi and axillary region where lymph nodes were removed.

Contraindications: This exercise is not appropriate if you have osteoporosis in the spine.

Equipment: Folded bath towel (optional; to sit on if your hamstrings are tight or you cannot bend your hips easily).

▶ **Start:**

Sit with left leg folded behind and right leg crossed in front.

▶ **Exercise:**

Inhale and reach left arm up and over your head to the right side.

Exhale as you laterally flex (bend) your body to the right side.

Inhale as you hold.

Exhale as you return arm to left side, sit back up, and return to start position.

Perform five to eight repetitions and then switch sides.

▶ **Be sure to:**

Keep your hips grounded. Be careful not to lift the hip on the same side as the working arm as you lift your arm up and over. Sit on a folded towel if your hamstrings (muscles in the back of your leg from the buttocks to knees) are tight.

▶ **Modifications:**

Sit in the tailor position if more comfortable.

For an added challenge:

Rest your nonworking hand on a weighted ball.

Phase 3

Regaining Strength, Power, and Endurance

If you haven't tried the modifications to add light hand weights to the below exercises in Phase 2, try them now.

- Arm Scissors

- Floating Arms

Remember to keep your wrists straight when holding weights.

If you have lymphedema or are at risk, progress slowly when using weights and do not increase the number of repetitions at the same time as you increase the weights. Be sure to monitor your arm(s) for any symptoms of lymphedema and to wear your sleeve and gauntlet as recommended by your therapist. If you feel heaviness or tightness, the progression may have been too rapid.

If you are undergoing a breast implant expander program or have undergone TRAM or DIEP flap reconstruction, do not use weights or resistance until cleared by your doctor, and eliminate or modify exercises as indicated.

Side Lying Rotator Cuff Push

Goal: To strengthen the rotator cuff, located in the back of the shoulder, enabling you to more easily perform tasks such as washing or blow-drying your hair.

Contraindications: Eliminate this exercise if it is too painful to lie on your affected side or arm. Be sure to wear your compression sleeve if recommended.

If you are undergoing a breast implant expander program or have undergone TRAM or DIEP flap reconstruction, do not use weights until cleared by your doctor. See modification.

If you have lower back problems, place a pad or towel between your knees.

If your side is sore, place a pad or towel under your elbow.

Equipment: Pad, small pillow, towel, or block under head, if needed, or if you experience discomfort resting your head on your arm.

Light hand weight (1–2 pounds).

▶ **Start:**

Lie on your side, with your back lined up against the edge of the mat, hips stacked, knees bent in a 90° angle and positioned at a 45° angle to the body.

Top arm is glued to your side with the elbow bent at 90°, and hand holding hand weight. Position bottom arm for comfort.

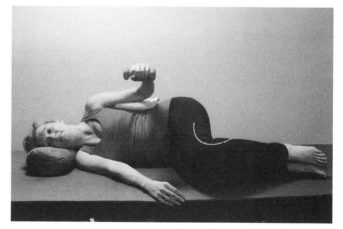

▶ **Exercise:**

Inhale to start and then exhale as you lift your top arm up and out to the side while keeping your elbow glued to your side.

Inhale as you hold.

Exhale and return to start.

Perform five to eight repetitions and then switch to the other side.

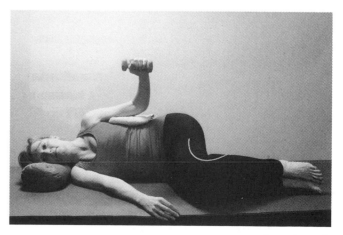

(continued)

▶ **Modifications: To lessen the intensity:**

- Do not use hand weights.

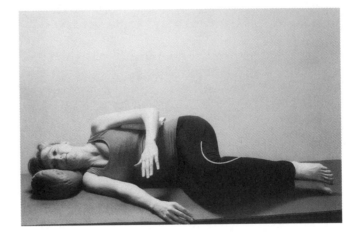

For an added challenge:

- Straighten legs.

Side Lying Chest Opener, Part 2

Goal: To open up the chest and underarm region, as well as stretch the neck, which is often tight after surgery.

Contraindications: Eliminate this exercise if it is too painful to lie on your affected side.

Be sure to wear your sleeve and gauntlet if recommended by your therapist.

If you are undergoing a breast implant expander program or have undergone TRAM or DIEP flap reconstruction, make sure that you are medically cleared for this exercise as well as for using weights.

If you have osteoporosis in the spine, do not perform this exercise.

If you have lower back problems, place a pad or towel between your knees.

Equipment: Pad, small pillow, towel, or block under head, if needed, or if you experience discomfort resting your head on your arm.

Large pillow (optional; to place under working arm to rest the arm as it stretches).

Light hand weight, 1 to 2 pounds (optional).

▶ **Start:**

Lie on your side, with your back lined up against the edge of the mat, hips stacked, knees bent in a 90° angle and positioned at a 45° angle to the body.

Bottom arm is positioned for comfort.

Top arm is stretched straight out, at shoulder height, holding weight (if using).

▶ **Exercise:**

Inhale to start, then exhale as you lift your top arm up toward the ceiling.

Inhale as you hold.

(continued)

Exhale as you extend your arm behind you, rotating your rib cage and moving your head to follow your hand with your gaze. Work within a pain-free zone.

Inhale as you hold. Having a pillow to rest your arm on can help you maintain this stretch and open up the chest as you breathe deeply.

Exhale to return to start position.

Perform five to eight repetitions then switch to the other side.

▶ Be sure to:

Only move to the point of discomfort, not pain.

Double Leg Kick

Goal: To strengthen your hamstrings, buttocks, and back muscles and stretch your chest, shoulder musculature, and quadriceps.

Contraindications: If you have a lower back injury, be sure to press your pubic bone into the mat. For added comfort, you can place a pillow under your hips.
If you have knee problems, limit the amount that you kick with your knees.

Equipment: None.

▶ Start:

Lie on your belly with your head turned to the right side.
Your pubic bone is pressed into the mat.
Legs are glued together with the toes pointed.
Hands are interlaced with the palms facing up and resting on your lower back.

▶ Exercise:

Inhale as you bend both knees and bring heels toward your buttocks. Pulse twice.
Exhale as you lower legs within a few inches of the floor while lifting your upper body off the mat and stretching your arms behind you.
Inhale and exhale as you lower legs and upper body to return to start position.
Rotate head to the left and repeat on the other side.

Swimming

Goal: To strengthen the shoulder and back muscles and improve posture. This exercise improves your bed mobility (to change positions in bed) and your ability to reach your arms up. It is also great for women with osteoporosis in the spine.

Contraindications: If you have back conditions such as stenosis, spondylolysis, or spondylolisthesis do not perform this exercise.

Equipment: Small pillow (optional; to place under forehead).

▶ **Start:**

Lie on your belly with both legs and arms extended. Your pubic bone is pressed into the mat.

▶ **Exercise:**

Inhale to start, then exhale as you lift your chest and head off the floor. Gaze is forward.

Inhale and exhale as you alternate lifting and lowering right arm/left leg with lifting and lowering left arm/right leg in a swimming motion.

▶ **Be sure to:**

Avoid any back pain. Start slowly with either arms or legs, but not both, if there is any back discomfort. Lift the legs only if there is shoulder discomfort. Keep your core still with no rocking from side to side.

▶ **Modifications:**

Place a pad or pillow under the pelvis if your back arches too much or you have abdominal discomfort.

Start by working arms or legs individually.

"I used Pilates to make me stronger than I was before diagnosis. My range of motion and the strength in my arms is better than before my double mastectomy. I never knew how weak I was until I started practicing Pilates. Pilates helped my core and upper body become so much stronger. I now have a better awareness of my body in general."

—*Beth Mast*

Side Lying Leg Series

Goal: To strengthen the gluteal, hip, and thigh muscles while stabilizing your core. These exercises will help make it easier for you to get out of bed when you are lying on your back or side.

Contraindications: With neck, shoulder, elbow, or wrist injuries, place your head on a pillow, block, or bolster.

If you have osteoporosis in the hips or other hip injuries, make very small circles and limit the height of your top leg lift to within your comfort zone.

Equipment: Pad, small pillow, towel, or block under head if needed, or if you experience discomfort when resting your head on your arm.

▶ Start:

Lie on your side, with your back lined up against the edge of the mat, hips and legs stacked, shoulders lined up, and toes pointed.

Top arm is pressed into the mat for stability.

Head is resting on bottom arm, which is extended.

Rib cage is lifted off the floor.

Top leg is lifted to hip height.

Gaze is forward, not at feet.

▶ Exercise:

#1: Circles

- Inhale and lift leg to hip height.
- Exhale as you make 10 small clockwise circles with your top leg. Reverse and make 10 counterclockwise circles.
- Return to start. Proceed to #2.

#2: Point and Flex

- Inhale and lift leg to hip height with pointed toes.
- Exhale and lower leg as you flex toes.

Perform five to six repetitions of this series on one side and then switch sides.

▶ **Be sure to:**

Keep pelvis stable and avoid tensing shoulders and neck. Keep shoulders and hips lined up without tilting forward or backward.

▶ **Modifications:**

Support rib cage on mat rather than keeping it lifted.

Bend the bottom knee for more support.

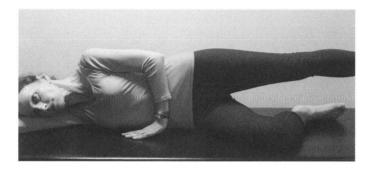

Hundred

Goal: To increase circulation and warm up the body. This exercise builds shoulder and abdominal strength, improves scapular mobility, and fosters lymphatic flow through deep breathing.

Contraindications: If you have osteoporosis in the spine, keep your head down on the mat.

Equipment: Pad, small pillow, towel, or block, if needed.

▶ Start:

Lie on your back with knees in tabletop.

Arms are long at your sides, raised to hip height.

Pelvis is level with the floor, in neutral, or imprinted if you have back problems.

▶ Exercise:

Inhale as you gently nod chin to chest.

Exhale as you lift upper body and shoulders off the floor while extending legs straight into a "V" position. Look at your belly button.

Pump your arms from your shoulder blades as you inhale for five beats, and then exhale for five beats. That is one cycle of 10.

Repeat the cycle 10 times for a complete Hundred or do as many cycles as you are able.

▶ Modifications:

The higher the legs the easier the exercise, while lowering the legs increases the difficulty.

To lessen the intensity:

- Decrease the number of repetitions.
- Keep your head down and feet on the floor and just pump the arms.

"This exercise was very helpful in building back my core."

—Grace T

Criss Cross, Feet Down

Goal: To strengthen the core, particularly the oblique muscles that twist your body, helping you to turn your torso as well as turn on your side when sleeping.

Contraindications: Do not perform this exercise if you have osteoporosis in the spine.

Equipment: Pad, small pillow, towel, or block under head, if needed.

▶ Start:

Lie on your back with both knees bent and feet on the ground, hip distance apart.
Pelvis is level with the floor, in neutral, or imprinted if you have back problems.
Hands are supporting the head, elbows stay wide but within your peripheral vision.

▶ Exercise:

Inhale to start, then exhale as you nod your chin to your chest, lift upper body and shoulders off the floor, and reach left elbow to right knee.
Inhale as you return to center, then exhale as you reach right elbow to left knee.
Inhale as you return to center.

▶ Modification: For an added challenge:

• Bring knees up to tabletop position.

▶ Be sure to:

Keep hip bones facing the ceiling with pelvis anchored to the mat and tailbone on the floor.

PART IV

TRAM or DIEP Flap Pilates Program

These exercises can be used after transverse rectus abdominis myocutaneous (TRAM) or deep inferior epigastric perforator (DIEP) flap breast reconstruction surgery. They are designed to be performed on an elevated table (such as a massage table), adjustable chair such as a recliner, or on your bed with a wedge under your head and upper back since at first it may be difficult for you to lie on the floor. If you are uncomfortable lying down, begin with the Chair Pilates program first (see Part V).

Follow all of your doctor's recommendations to ensure the safety of your flap sites in both the chest area and abdominal region. In addition, you may still have drains by your arms and hips, making it difficult to lie down. Listen to your body; healing is different for all.

If you are at risk for lymphedema, wear a sleeve and gauntlet (glove) if recommended by your health care professional. Progress slowly when using weights and do not increase the number of repetitions at the same time that you increase the weights. Start with light weights such as 1 pound.

If you have back issues, always use an imprinted spine, not a neutral spine, for all exercises.

If you have osteoporosis or osteopenia in the spine, avoid flexing or turning your back.

If you are undergoing chemotherapy, adhere to your physician's recommendations and precautions.

Phase 1: Protective Phase

These exercises are safe to do postsurgery with drains in place, and can be continued after your drains are removed. Do three to five repetitions of each of these exercises, on each side of the body. This phase will last approximately four to six weeks, until you feel comfortable progressing to more difficult exercises and are medically cleared. The exercises should feel easier and there should be no discomfort before moving on to the next phase. The exercises should be done in their presented order to establish a daily routine.

The goal of this phase is to ensure tissue healing without sacrificing range of motion and flexibility of the chest and arms. You will most likely be in a flexed (bent) position to protect the abdominal region and chest at this time. Remember not to roll or twist your trunk or place pressure over your chest. Try to use your hands for bathing, dressing, or washing as long as you don't bring your arm past 90°.

When you move on to Phase 2 and Phase 3, use the exercises in Phase 1 as your warm-up.

- Pelvic Tilts: Neutral and Imprinted Spine

- Breathing

- Scapula Elevation and Depression

- Scapula Protraction and Retraction

- Bridging

- Cane Raises

Phase 2: Return to Function

After your drains are removed, healing is proceeding well, and you are comfortable with the Phase 1 exercises (6–8 weeks postsurgery), add the exercises in Phase 2 to your routine for at least two weeks. By now, you should be able to lie supine. Usually, you can start the Swan six weeks postsurgery if cleared by your physician. Begin with three to five repetitions of each exercise, gradually increasing to five to eight.

- Heel Slides

- Knee Stirs

- Cat Stretch

- Swan

Phase 3: Regaining Strength, Power, and Endurance

Once you are able to do the exercises in Phases 1 and 2 without pain or discomfort, and have a doctor's clearance, add the following to your routine (8–10 weeks postsurgery). Begin with three to five repetitions of each exercise, gradually increasing to five to eight. At this point in time, you should be able to transition down to a mat. If not, it is highly recommended that you speak to your medical provider regarding rehabilitation.

- Hundred, Feet Down

- Criss Cross, Feet Down

- Side Lying Leg Circles

- Single Leg Stretch

- Swimming

- Alternate Arm and Leg Lift

For all exercises, five to eight repetitions maximum is recommended. However, everyone is different and you should work within your own tolerance. How you feel can vary from day to day, so please be gentle with yourself.

Please remember:

- Stretch before and after Pilates or take a warm shower to warm up the body.

- A pad, small pillow, towel, or block under your head can help place your head in the proper position when side lying or supine.

- A medium-sized ball between your knees will help you to activate the pelvic floor and transverse abdominis muscles so that you can feel the muscles working. You will feel a flutter in the abdominal region when the transverse abdominis muscle is activated. However, sensation may be impaired after surgery in the abdominal region as well as the chest.

- Always alternate arm and leg exercises to prevent fatigue, and rest when needed.

- Drink plenty of water to stay hydrated.

- A neutral spine is a goal to be achieved. Due to the surgery you may only be able to imprint at first.

What Is Good Posture in Supine (Lying on Your Back)?

Before starting mat Pilates, do a body scan to ensure that you are starting correctly.

Questions to ask yourself:

- Are my feet aligned with my knees with weight equally on toes as well as heels? Are my toes forward?

- Is the center of my kneecap aligned with my middle toe? Is there equal weight on both feet?

- Are my knees aligned with my hips? (Draw an imaginary line from your hips to your knees.)

- Is my pelvis level with the floor, in neutral, or is my spine imprinted if I have any back issues?

- Are both hip bones pointing toward the ceiling?

- Are my arms resting at my side?

- Are my shoulders level and neutral, not lifted up to my ears?

- Are my shoulder blades in neutral (placed on the mat) so they are not pushed forward?

- Is my rib cage soft and down?

- Is my chin in and my neck long?

- Are my head and neck aligned with my spine or is my neck arched or my head too far forward? (If you are out of alignment or your neck hurts when lying on your back, use a pad, small pillow, towel, or block under your head to achieve the proper position.)

Remember, if you are unable to lie on your back on the floor, do the exercises in a reclining chair or in bed with a wedge under your head and upper back. If these positions are uncomfortable, do the chair Pilates program.

Phase 1

Protective Phase

Pelvic Tilts: Neutral and Imprinted Spine

Goal: To learn how to find a neutral pelvis, a neutral spine, and an imprinted spine.

Neutral spine is the natural position of the spine when all three curves of the spine—cervical (neck), thoracic (middle), and lumbar (lower)—are present and in good alignment. This is the strongest position of the spine and supports all movement, reducing the risk of injury. This is the ideal position of the spine in most Pilates exercises but it may be difficult to achieve after surgery. If you are unable to achieve neutral spine, imprint your spine.

An imprinted spine is the lower back flat against the floor, with no gaps. Imagine sinking your lower back into sand, tilting your pelvis toward your nose. Imprinting helps to protect the back in Pilates exercises that require both legs to be raised off the floor, and in any exercise if you have back problems. The position of your pelvis determines the position of your spine.

Contraindications: If you have any back problems, always use an imprinted spine for all exercises.

Equipment: Pad, small pillow, towel, or block under head, if needed.

Medium-sized ball (optional; squeezing the ball between your knees will help to activate the pelvic floor and transverse abdominis muscles).

▶ Start:

Lie on your back with both knees bent and feet on the ground, hip distance apart.

Place the ring and little fingers of both hands on your hip bones, and make a heart with your index fingers pointed toward the pubic bone. Your thumbs are pointed toward the belly button.

▶ Exercise:

Gently tilt your pelvis forward and backward several times until both hands are on the same plane and parallel to the floor. This is your neutral pelvis. When your pelvis is in neutral, your spine is in neutral.

- Neutral = Thumbs and index fingers should be on the same plane and halfway between the two positions

From neutral, gently tilt your pelvis to your nose so your back is flat against the floor. Your thumbs will be lower than your index fingers. Now your spine is imprinted.

(continued)

- Imprinted = Gently tilt pelvis to nose. Your thumbs will be lower than your index fingers. This is used to support the lower back during exercises where the legs are raised off the floor, or with certain back conditions. Think *lower back to the floor using your abdominal muscles.* Do not squeeze your buttocks or thighs. They should stay relaxed.

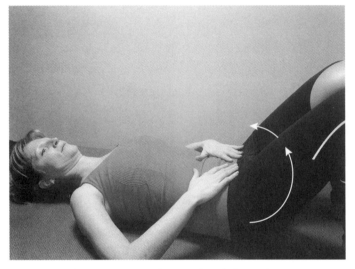

Note: Model is in neutral. To imprint, follow the arrows.

Breathing

Goal: To learn the Pilates breathing method of rib cage breathing, relax the chest area and prepare the body for exercise. This breathing helps to stretch the tight pectoralis major muscle after surgery as well as learning how to activate the transverse abdominis. Always come back to this breathing if you experience any discomfort.

Contraindications: None.

Equipment: Pad, small pillow, towel, or block under head, if needed.
Medium-sized ball (optional; squeezing the ball between your knees will help to activate the pelvic floor and transverse abdominis muscles).

▶ Start:

Lie on your back with both knees bent and feet on the floor, hip distance apart.
Pelvis is level with the floor, in neutral, if you are able, or imprinted, especially if you have back problems.
Hands on rib cage.

▶ Exercise:

Inhale to "smell the roses" and feel your rib cage expand to the front, sides, and back. This is called rib cage breathing.
Exhale "to blow out the candles" as you feel your rib cage grow smaller. This will help to activate the muscles and promote relaxation.

▶ Be sure to:

Rise from the floor slowly. Many of us are not used to breathing deeply so you may feel a bit dizzy after performing deep breathing.

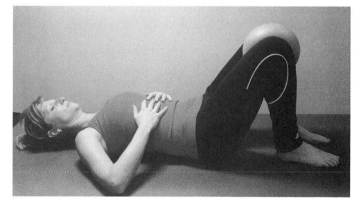

Scapula Elevation and Depression

Goal: To warm up the scapular muscles, including the upper and middle trapezius, and prepare for shoulder exercises.

Contraindications: None.

Equipment: Pad, small pillow, towel, or block under head, if needed.
Medium-sized ball (optional; squeezing the ball between your knees will help to activate the pelvic floor and transverse abdominis muscles and prevent your knees from collapsing in).

▶ Start:

Lie on your back with both knees bent and feet on the ground, hip distance apart.

Pelvis is level with the floor, in neutral, if you are able, or imprinted, especially if you have back problems.

Arms are long at your sides.

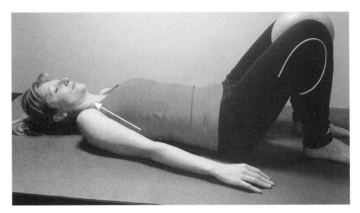

Elevation

▶ Exercise:

Inhale as you slide your shoulder blades (back wing bones) up toward your ears (elevation).

Exhale as you slide your shoulder blades down (depression). Imagine your shoulder blades are sliding gently into your back pockets.

Depression

▶ Be sure to:

Keep both shoulders on the mat as you slide them up and down. Don't allow your shoulders to round forward.

Scapula Protraction and Retraction

Goal: To warm up the shoulders in preparation for movement, as well as strengthen the muscles around the scapula (shoulder blade), including the serratus anterior and rhomboids, that are necessary for proper shoulder movement.

Contraindications: None.

Equipment: Pad, small pillow, towel, or block under head, if needed.
Medium-sized ball (optional; squeezing the ball between your knees will help to activate the pelvic floor and transverse abdominis muscles and prevent your knees from collapsing in).

▶ **Start:**

Lie on your back with both knees bent and feet on the ground, hip distance apart.

Pelvis is level with the floor, in neutral, if you are able, or imprinted, especially if you have back problems.

Arms and fingertips are reaching toward the ceiling at no more than a 90° angle to your shoulders.

Protraction

▶ **Exercise:**

Inhale and reach fingertips toward the ceiling (shoulder blades will lift off the mat). This is protraction.

Exhale and bring your shoulder blades together (not too hard) as you imagine you are gently cracking a walnut between your shoulder blades. This is retraction.

Retraction

(continued)

▶ **Modification: For an added challenge:**

- Stretch a resistance band between your hands.

Pilates helps me to build strength and confidence little by little.

—*Grace T.*

Bridging

Goal: To warm up the spine as well as your hamstrings and gluteal muscles. This exercise will help make it easier to put on your underwear and pants and reposition yourself in bed.

Contraindications: Check with your physician to make sure that this exercise is safe for you to do when recovering with drains in place.

Equipment: Pad, small pillow, towel, or block under head, if needed.
Medium-sized ball (optional; squeezing the ball between your knees will help to activate the pelvic floor and transverse abdominis muscles and prevent your knees from collapsing in).

▶ **Start:**

Lie on your back with both knees bent and feet on the ground, hip distance apart.
Pelvis is level with the floor, in neutral, if you are able, or imprinted, especially if you have back problems.
Arms are long at your sides.

▶ **Exercise:**

Inhale to start and then exhale as you tilt your pelvis toward your nose to imprint your spine.

Push off through your heels and lift your spine off the mat one vertebra at a time. You will start moving the lower back, middle back, and then upper back off the mat.

Inhale as you hold this position at the point where you can remain still, without any movement of your pelvis. The upper part of both your shoulder blades should remain on the mat.

Exhale as you return to the start position by gradually bringing the upper back, middle back, and lower back gently down to the mat, vertebra by vertebra, to your neutral or imprinted pelvis. Think of rolling the spine slowly down to the floor.

▶ **Be sure to:**

Keep both shoulder blades on the mat. Do not let the pelvis rock forward and backward or side to side.

Cane Raises

Goal: To increase range of motion and stability in the shoulder, necessary for putting on garments or reaching overhead as well as stretching the latissimus dorsi muscle, which is often tight after surgery.

Contraindications: Only move your arms to 90°.
If you still have drains, only proceed within your physician's guidelines.

Equipment: Pad, small pillow, towel, or block under head, if needed.
Medium-sized ball (optional; squeezing the ball between your knees will help to activate the pelvic floor and transverse abdominis muscles and prevent your knees from collapsing in).
Cane, pole, towel, or umbrella.

▶ Start:

Lie on your back with both knees bent and feet on the ground, hip distance apart.
Pelvis is level with the floor, in neutral, if you are able, or imprinted if you have back problems.
Arms are at hips, hands holding the cane, towel, pole, or umbrella.

▶ Exercise:

Inhale to start as you imprint your shoulder blades on the mat, and then exhale to lift cane until arms are at a 90° angle to your shoulders. Inhale as you hold.
Exhale as you return your arms to the starting position.

▶ Be sure to:

Keep your shoulder blades on the mat. Don't let your rib cage pop out or your back arch while lifting your arms above your head. Work within your comfort zone.

Phase 2

Return to Function

Heel Slides

Goal: To gain stability in your pelvic region, activate your transverse abdominis, and improve hamstring flexibility.

Contraindications: None.

Equipment: Pad, small pillow towel, or block under head, if needed.
Small toning balls under the toes to help with movement or small towel under the ball of the foot to facilitate movement (optional).

▶ Start:

Lie on your back with both knees bent and feet on the ground, hip distance apart.

Pelvis is level with the floor, in neutral, if you are able, or imprinted if you have back problems.

Hands are resting on pelvis.

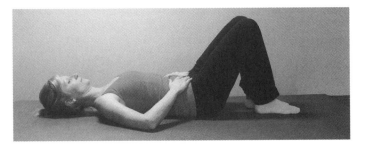

▶ Exercise:

Inhale to start, and then exhale to press the right heel away to extend the leg out. Inhale to return to start position.

Perform all repetitions on one leg, and then switch. When this is mastered, alternate sides.

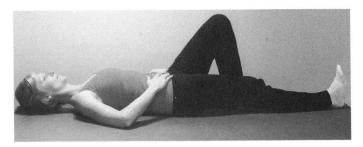

▶ Be sure to:

Keep the pelvis stable; do not let the pelvis rock. Both hips should be facing toward the ceiling as you extend the leg out.

Only go as far as is comfortable for you. If you have tight hamstrings, you may not be able to extend the legs all the way out.

Knee Stirs

Goal: To relieve tension in hip joints, increase hip flexibility and help you to learn how to stabilize your pelvis while moving your legs.

Contraindications: None.

Equipment: Pad, small pillow, towel, or block under head, if needed.

▶ Start:

Lie on your back with both knees bent and feet on the mat, hip distance apart.

Pelvis is level with the floor, in neutral, if you are able, or imprinted if you have back problems.

Arms are long at your sides.

▶ Exercise:

Inhale to start, then exhale to lift right leg so that the thigh is perpendicular to the floor and the shin is parallel to the floor. Left foot remains on the floor.

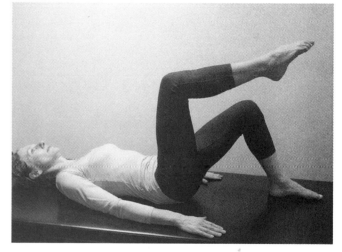

Inhale to circle the right leg inward toward your left leg. Keep the circles as small as a cake plate to maintain your pelvic stability. Perform five to eight repetitions and then reverse the circle outward.

Complete all repetitions with one leg and then switch legs.

▶ Be sure to:

Keep your pelvis stable. Your tailbone should remain on the floor. As you circle your working leg, check to make sure that your hips are not rocking. Your hips should be facing the ceiling at all times.

Cat Stretch

Goal: To stretch the lower back, which is often tight after surgery.

Contraindications: This exercise is not appropriate if you have osteoporosis in the spine or lymphedema. Read modification below.
If you have knee issues, place a pad or towel under your knees.

Equipment: None.

▶ **Start:**

On hands and knees with your back to the ceiling.
Hands are placed under your shoulders.
Knees are hip distance apart, under the hips, with the tops of your feet resting on the mat.
Pelvis is parallel to the floor, in neutral.

▶ **Exercise:**

Inhale to start, then exhale as you draw your belly in. Gradually bring each vertebra in your back up, arching like a cat. Move from the lower back, to middle back, to upper back and head.
Inhale as you hold.
Exhale and return to start position.

▶ **Be sure to:**

Keep the head in alignment with your spine as you straighten your back from the arched position.

▶ **Modification: To lessen the challenge or if you have lymphedema:**

- Rest hands on a table or countertop with both knees bent rather than bearing your whole body weight on hands.

Swan

Goal: To strengthen the scapular and back muscles, improve shoulder mobility, and prepare shoulders for weight bearing activity.

Contraindications: If you have lymphedema in the arm, this exercise is not recommended; the arm must be prepared for weight bearing. See modification.

Equipment: Foam roller, weighted balls, or towel.

▶ Start:

Lie on your belly with arms stretched over your head and elbows bent slightly. Heels of hands on foam roller, balls, or towel.
Rest your forehead on the mat.
Legs are extended on the mat, hip distance apart.
Pubic bone is pressed into mat.

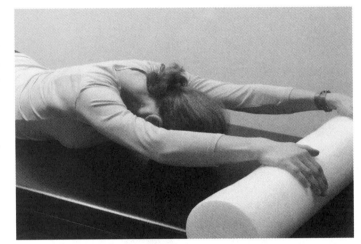

▶ Exercise:

Inhale to start and then exhale as you press hands into foam roller, balls, or towel as you lift your head and back as one unit off the mat. Pubic bone remains on the mat while shoulder blades slide away from ears as you lift your upper body off the mat.
Inhale as you hold and gaze forward.
Exhale and return to start.

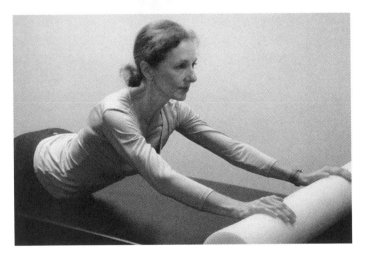

▶ **Be sure to:**

Avoid pain in your lower back. If you feel pain, you may have lifted your body too high. Reduce the height that you lift your back, or place a pad or pillow under your hip bones. Eliminate if pain persists.

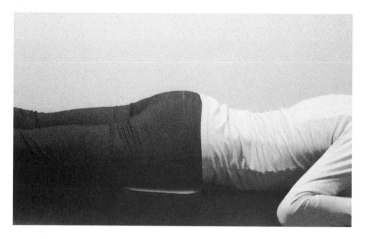

▶ **Modification: To lessen the intensity or if you have lymphedema:**

- Keep both elbows bent on the floor with hands flat so trunk does not lift as high and the back is protected. You may still need to protect the abdominal region with a pillow or pad.

Phase 3

Regaining Strength, Power, and Endurance

Hundred, Feet Down

Goal: To strengthen the abdominal muscles and scapular muscles, such as the serratus anterior and latissimus dorsi, and improve shoulder strength.

Contraindications: If you have osteoporosis in the spine, do this exercise with head down; do not lift your head off the mat.

Equipment: Pad, small pillow, towel, or block under head, if needed.
Medium-sized ball (optional; squeezing the ball between your knees will help to activate the pelvic floor and transverse abdominis muscles and prevent your knees from collapsing in).

▶ Start:

Lie on your back with both knees bent and feet on the ground, hip distance apart.
Pelvis is level with the floor, in neutral, if you are able, or imprinted, especially if you have back problems.
Arms are long at your sides.

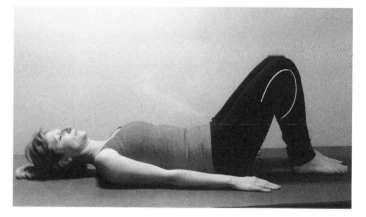

▶ Exercise:

Inhale as you gently nod your chin to your chest.
Exhale as you lift upper body and shoulders off the floor while stretching your arms toward your feet. Look at your belly button and keep your neck relaxed.
Pump your arms from the back of your shoulders as you inhale for five beats and then exhale for five beats. That is one cycle of 10.

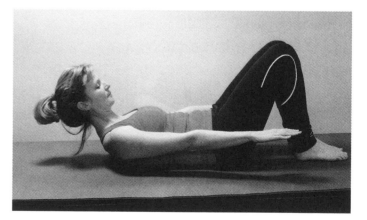

Repeat the cycle 10 times for a complete Hundred or do as many cycles as you are able.

▶ Be sure to:

Make the movement come from the scapular muscles, not the elbows or head. You can support your head with one hand if necessary to protect the neck.

Criss Cross, Feet Down

Goal: To strengthen the core, particularly the oblique muscles that twist your body, helping you to turn your torso as well as turn on your side when sleeping.

Contraindications: Do not perform this exercise if you have osteoporosis in the spine.

Equipment: Pad, small pillow, towel, or block under head, if needed.

▶ Start:

Lie on your back with both knees bent and feet on the ground, hip distance apart.

Pelvis is level with the floor, in neutral, if you are able, or imprinted, especially if you have back problems.

Hands are supporting the head, elbows stay wide but within your peripheral vision.

▶ Exercise:

Inhale to start, then exhale as you nod your chin to your chest, lift upper body and shoulders off the floor, and reach left elbow to right knee.

Inhale as you return to center, then exhale as you reach right elbow to left knee.

Inhale as you return to center.

▶ Be sure to:

Keep hip bones facing the ceiling, with pelvis anchored to the mat and tailbone on the floor.

▶ Modification: For an added challenge:

- Lift legs to table top or ceiling

Side Lying Leg Circles

Goal: To strengthen gluteal, hip, and thigh muscles while stabilizing your core. These exercises will help make it easier for you to get out of bed when you are lying on your back or side.

Contraindications: With neck, shoulder, elbow, or wrist injuries, place your head on a pillow, block, or bolster.

If you have osteoporosis in the hips, make very small circles.

If you have hip injuries, limit the height of your top leg lift to within your comfort zone.

Equipment: Pad, small pillow, towel, or block under head, if needed, or if you experience discomfort when resting your head on your arm.

▶ Start:

Lie on your side with your back lined up against the edge of the mat, hips and legs stacked, shoulders lined up, and toes pointed.

Your top arm is pressed into the mat for stability.

Head is resting on bottom arm, which is extended.

Rib cage is lifted off the floor.

Gaze is forward, not at feet.

▶ Exercise:

Inhale and lift leg to hip height.

Exhale as you make eight to ten small (8–10 inch) clockwise circles with your top leg. Reverse to make eight to ten counterclockwise circles.

Perform five to six repetitions on one side and then switch sides.

▶ Be sure to:

Keep pelvis stable and avoid tensing shoulders and neck. Keep shoulders and hips lined up without tilting forward or backward.

(continued)

▶ **Modification: To lessen the intensity:**

- Support rib cage on mat rather than keeping it lifted.

- Place body at a slight angle from the hip, with feet reaching to the opposite corner of the mat.

- Bend the bottom knee for more support.

Single Leg Stretch

Goal: To maintain flexibility in your hips and legs and strengthen the abdominals.

Contraindications: If you have osteoporosis in the spine, do not lift your head off of the mat, and eliminate arm movements. See modification.

Equipment: Pad, small pillow, towel, or block under head, if needed.

▶ **Start:**

Lie on your back with knees in tabletop.
Pelvis is imprinted (tilt your pelvis toward your nose).
Arms are long at your sides.

▶ **Exercise:**

Inhale to start, then exhale as you nod your chin to your chest and lift upper body and shoulders off the floor.
Inhale, then exhale as you bring your right knee to your chest and extend your left leg at a 45° angle.
Inhale, then exhale as you bring your left knee to your chest and extend your right leg at a 45° angle.

▶ **Be sure to:**

Imprint the pelvis to protect the back and keep your pelvis stable. Do not rock your body from side to side as you switch legs.

(continued)

▶ **Modifications: To lessen the intensity:**

- Rest head on mat and eliminate arm movements. Just move the legs. Be sure to keep the pelvis imprinted.

For an added challenge:

- Only move the legs and lower the extended leg.

 "I believe strongly that being active and exercising regularly are the keys to quicker recovery from surgery. While energy levels are severely affected by chemotherapy, the best thing I did for myself was to exercise."

—*Bonnie O.*

Swimming

Goal: To strengthen the shoulder and back muscles and improve posture. This exercise improves your bed mobility (to change positions in bed) and your ability to reach your arms up. It is also great for women with osteoporosis in the spine.

Contraindications: If you have back conditions such as stenosis, spondylolysis, or spondylolisthesis do not perform this exercise.

Equipment: Small pillow (optional; to place under forehead).

▶ **Start:**
Lie on your belly with both legs and arms extended.
Your pubic bone is pressed into the mat.

▶ **Exercise:**
Inhale to start, then exhale as you lift your chest and head off the floor. Gaze is forward.

Inhale and exhale as you alternate lifting and lowering your right arm and left leg with lifting and lowering your left arm and right leg in a swimming motion.

(continued)

▶ **Be sure to:**

Avoid any back pain. Start slowly with either arms or legs, but not both, if there is any back discomfort. Lift the legs only if there is shoulder discomfort. Keep your core still with no rocking from side to side.

▶ **Modifications:**

- Place a pad or pillow under the pelvis if your back arches too much or there is abdominal discomfort.
- Start by working your arms or legs individually.

Alternate Arm and Leg Lift

Goal: To strengthen your core, lower back, and gluteal muscles. This is a great exercise for women with osteoporosis in the spine.

Contraindications: Make sure to wear your sleeve and gauntlet for this exercise if you are at risk for lymphedema, and warm up beforehand. You can hold weights in the hand on the floor to keep the wrists straight. Avoid this exercise if it causes too much discomfort in the wrist or hands. If you cannot perform a neutral spine for any reason, do not perform this exercise.

Equipment: Pad (optional; to place under knees to increase comfort level).

▶ Start:

On hands and knees with your back to the ceiling. Your hands are placed under your shoulders.
Knees are hip distance apart under your hips and the tops of your feet rest on the mat.
Pelvis is parallel to the floor, in neutral.
Your neck is in line with your spine and eyes gaze downward.

▶ Exercise:

Inhale to start and exhale as you lift right arm to shoulder height and left leg to hip height.
Inhale as you hold.
Exhale to lower arm and leg to start position.
Complete repetitions with right arm and left leg and then switch to left arm and right leg.

▶ Be sure to:

Keep hip bones facing the floor and back stable, without twisting or turning.

(*continued*)

▶ **Modifications: For an added challenge:**

- Add light hand weights (1–2 pounds) or weighted balls to the arm that you lift. Only use weights if cleared by your doctor.

To lessen the intensity:

- Perform fewer repetitions.
- Lift only one arm or leg at a time.

PART V

Chair Pilates Program

This chair Pilates program is ideal if you have difficulty moving from standing to lying on the floor. In addition, it is excellent for working the arms and back if you have osteoporosis or poor balance. This is a good place to start after all breast cancer surgeries as well as during treatment if endurance is not good.

Choose a stable chair without arms for maximum benefit. Be sure to sit at the edge of the chair to optimize your posture.

You can use a pillow behind your back if you are recovering from transverse rectus abdominis muscle (TRAM) or deep inferior epigastric perforators (DIEP) flap surgery, when sitting upright may not be possible.

If you are at risk for lymphedema, wear a sleeve and gauntlet (glove) if recommended by your health care professional. Progress slowly when using weights and do not increase the number of repetitions at the same time that you increase the weights. Start with light weights such as 1 pound.

If you are undergoing a breast implant expander program, or have undergone TRAM or DIEP flap reconstruction, do not use weights or resistance bands until cleared by your doctor, and eliminate or modify exercises as indicated.

If you have back issues, always use an imprinted spine, not a neutral spine, for all exercises.

If you have osteoporosis or osteopenia in the spine, avoid flexing your spine.

If you are undergoing chemotherapy, adhere to your physician's recommendations and precautions.

Phase 1: Protective Phase

These exercises are safe to do postsurgery with drains in place, and can be continued after your drains are removed, with medical clearance. Do three to five repetitions of each of these exercises, on each side of the body. This phase will last approximately four weeks, until you feel comfortable progressing to more difficult exercises and are medically cleared. The exercises should feel easier and there should be no discomfort before moving on to the next phase. The exercises should be done in the order in which they are presented to establish a daily routine. The goal of this phase is to ensure tissue healing without sacrificing range of motion and flexibility of the chest and arm. When you move on to Phase 2 and Phase 3, use the exercises in Phase 1 as your warm-up.

- Pelvic Tilts: Imprint and Release

- Breathing with Band

- Scapula Elevation and Depression

- Scapula Protraction and Retraction

- Shoulder Rolls

- Hip Hinge

Phase 2: Return to Function

Once you are comfortable with the Phase 1 exercises, add the exercises in Phase 2 to your routine for two to four weeks. Begin with three to five repetitions of each exercise, gradually increasing to five to eight.

- Hundred

- Marching

- Arm Series

    Hug a Tree

    Arm Scissors

    Open the Door

    Up "W"

- Heel Slides

Phase 3: Regaining Strength, Power, and Endurance

Once you are able to do the exercises in Phases 1 and 2 without pain or discomfort (approximately 6–8 weeks postsurgery), add the following to your routine. Begin with three to five repetitions of each exercise, gradually increasing to five to eight.

- Marching with Arm Lifts

- Marching with Arm Scissors

- Rowing with Band

For all exercises, five to eight repetitions maximum is recommended. However, everyone is different and you should work within your own tolerance. How you feel can vary from day to day, so please be gentle with yourself.

Please remember:

- Stretch before and after Pilates or take a warm shower to warm up the body.

- A pillow can be placed behind the back for support if you are unable to sit upright in this position without pain or discomfort.

- A medium-sized ball between your knees will help you to activate the pelvic floor and transverse abdominis muscles so that you can feel the muscles working. You will feel a flutter in the abdominal region when the transverse abdominis muscle is activated. However, sensation may be impaired after surgery in the abdominal region as well as the chest.

- Always alternate arm and leg exercises to prevent fatigue, and rest when needed.

- Drink plenty of water to stay hydrated.

What is Good Seated Posture?

Sitting in a slouched posture places a lot of pressure on the lower back discs. Begin every exercise with your spine and pelvis in proper alignment and in neutral, if able, to ensure that you do the exercises correctly.
Questions to ask yourself:

- Am I seated on the edge of a chair?

- Are my feet flat on the ground with weight equally distributed on both feet and feet hip distance apart while pointing straight ahead?

- Are my hips at a 90° angle?

- Are my knees hip distance apart? Is my pelvis in neutral?

  Place your ring and little fingers on hip bones and thumbs above your belly button to make a heart. Move pelvis forward (back arched) and backward until thumbs are level with ring and little fingers. This is neutral.

- Am I sitting up on my sitz bones?

  To maintain a neutral pelvis, you should feel your sitz bones sharp against the chair. To find your sitz bones, place your hands palm up underneath your buttocks; they are the most prominent bones. If you are sitting properly the sitz bones will feel pointy in your hands. When you are slouched the sitz bones feel flat. If you are arched forward too much or slouched all of your weight comes into the back of your thighs.

- Is my rib cage over my hips?

- Are my ears over my shoulders?

- Are my shoulders over my hips?

- Are my eyes gazing straight ahead?

- Do I feel an imaginary string lifting me up through the top of my head?

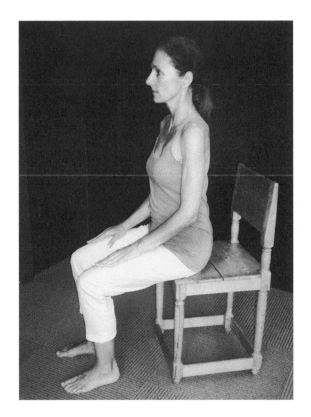

Phase 1

Protective Phase

Pelvic Tilts: Imprint and Release

Goal: To activate the core muscles, loosen up the spine, and learn how to imprint your pelvis while seated.

Contraindications: None.

Equipment: Chair without arms.

▶ **Start:**

Sit on edge of chair.

Pelvis is in neutral, or imprinted if you have back problems.
Your rib cage is over your hips.

Eyes gaze forward.

Ring and little fingers are placed in front of your hip bones, with index fingers pointing down and thumbs by rib cage above belly button.

▶ **Exercise:**

Inhale, then exhale to gently tip pelvis away (imprint) toward the chair (the lower back is rounded and activated). Fingers are higher than thumbs.

Inhale as you hold, then exhale as you return to start (neutral position). Thumbs and fingers should be on the same plane.

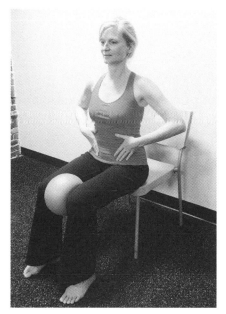

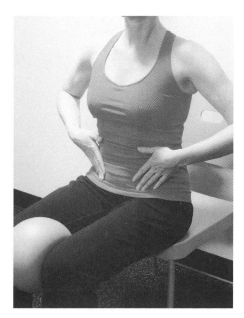

Neutral

Imprinted

Breathing with Band

Goal: To learn the Pilates breathing method of rib cage breathing, prepare the body for exercise, and promote relaxation. You can always return to this exercise when you feel pain.

Contraindication: If you are undergoing a breast implant expander program or have undergone TRAM or DIEP flap reconstruction, eliminate the resistance band and place hands on rib cage.

Equipment: Chair without arms.
Exercise band.

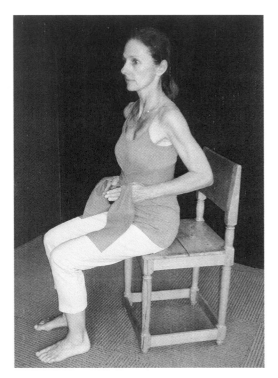

▶ Start:

Sit on edge of chair, with spine and pelvis in neutral, or imprinted if you have back problems.
Your rib cage is over your hips.
Eyes gaze forward.
Wrap band around your back by the bra line and cross in front of the body holding the ends with both hands.

▶ Exercise:

Inhale to "smell the roses" and feel your rib cage expand (band will expand) to the front, sides, and back.
Exhale to "blow out the candles" as you feel your rib cage grow smaller.

Scapula Elevation and Depression

Goal: To relieve tension in the neck, shoulders, and upper back and activate the scapular muscles.

Contraindications: None.

Equipment: Chair without arms.
Medium-sized ball (optional; squeezing the ball between your knees will help to activate the pelvic floor and transverse abdominis muscles and prevent your knees from collapsing in).

▶ **Start:**

Sit on edge of chair.

Pelvis is in neutral, or imprinted if you have back problems.

Your rib cage is over your hips.

Eyes gaze forward.

Arms are at your sides and reaching for the floor.

▶ **Exercise:**

Inhale as you lift shoulder blades to ears.

Exhale, as you drop shoulder blades down while reaching your fingertips to the floor.

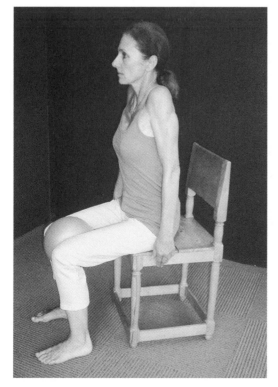

Elevation

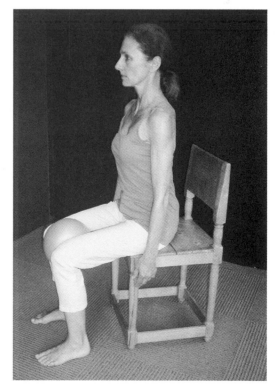

Depression

Scapula Protraction and Retraction

Goal: To warm up the shoulder muscles and encourage proper shoulder movement.

Contraindications: None.

Equipment: Chair without arms.

Medium-sized ball (optional; squeezing the ball between your knees will help to activate the pelvic floor and transverse abdominis muscles and prevent your knees from collapsing in).

▶ **Start:**

Sit on edge of chair.

Pelvis is in neutral, or imprinted if you have back problems.

Your rib cage is over your hips.

Eyes gaze forward.

Arms are lifted to shoulder height with palms facing in.

▶ **Exercise:**

Inhale and reach the fingertips away from you as if you are hugging a child. This is protraction.

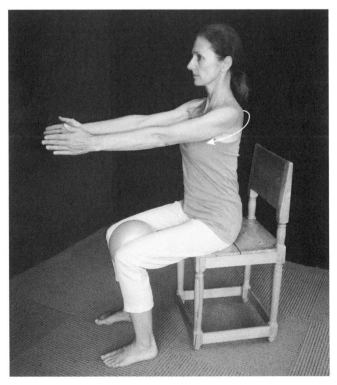

Protraction

Exhale as you gently pull shoulder blades back toward one another. This is retraction.

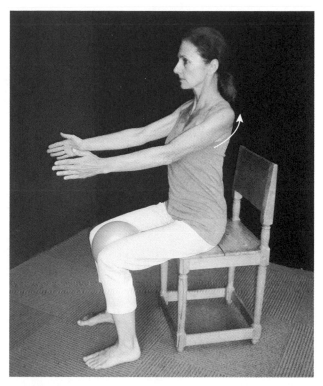

Retraction

▶ **Modification: For an added challenge:**

- Add 1 to 2 pound hand weights. If you are undergoing a breast implant expander program or have undergone TRAM or DIEP flap reconstruction, do not use weights until medically cleared.

Shoulder Rolls

Goal: To warm up the shoulder muscles in preparation for movement.

Contraindications: None.

Equipment: Chair without arms.

Medium-sized ball (optional; squeezing the ball between your knees will help to activate the pelvic floor and transverse abdominis muscles and prevent your knees from collapsing in).

▶ **Start:**

Sit on edge of chair.

Pelvis is in neutral, or imprinted if have back problems.

Your rib cage is over your hips.

Eyes gaze forward.

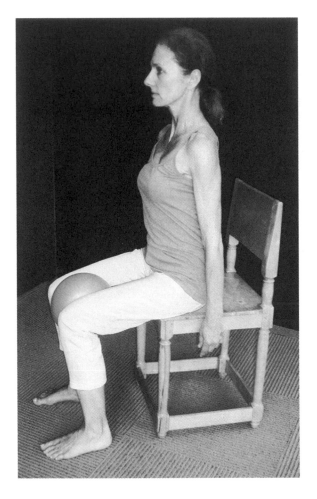

▶ **Exercise:**

Inhale as you elevate shoulders to ears and roll shoulders back.

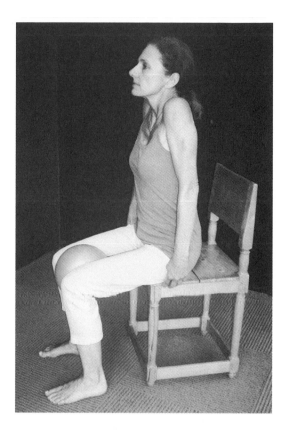

Exhale, as you drop shoulders down. Imagine making a circle with your shoulders toward your back. Think shoulders up, around, and down. Keep the circles small if it is painful, and do the deep breathing exercises.

Perform five to eight repetitions and then reverse direction, going forward toward your head.

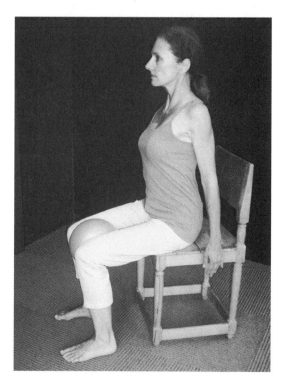

Hip Hinge

Goal: To strengthen the legs and core, making getting up from a chair or off the toilet easier. This is an excellent exercise to learn how to bend from the hips if you have osteoporosis in the spine and how to weight-bear on your feet while getting up from a seated position.

Contraindications: If you have peripheral neuropathy, wear sturdy shoes.

Equipment: Chair without arms.

▶ **Start:**

Sit on edge of chair.

Pelvis is in neutral, or imprinted if you have back problems.

Your rib cage is over your hips.

Eyes gaze forward.

Heels of hands are on hips.

▶ **Exercise:**

Inhale, then exhale as you bend forward and flex at the hips. Bear weight onto the heels of your feet to push yourself up to standing.

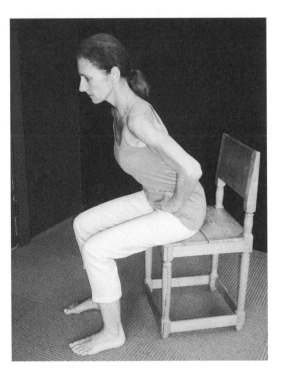

Bear weight onto the heels as you bend knees to sit back down at the edge of the chair.

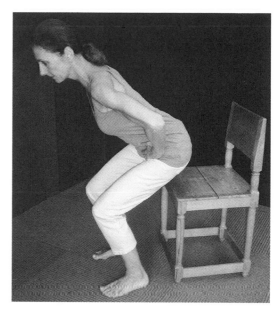

▶ **Modification:**

If your legs are weak, place palms down on thighs to assist.

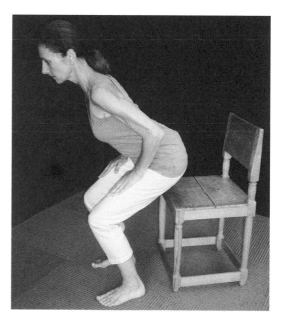

Phase 2

Return to Function

Hundred

Goal: To increase strength of the shoulders and abdominals as well as promote lymphatic drainage.

Contraindications: None.

Equipment: Chair without arms.
Medium-sized ball (optional; squeezing the ball between your knees will help to activate the pelvic floor and transverse abdominis muscles and prevent your knees from collapsing in).

▶ Start:
Sit on edge of chair.
Pelvis is in neutral, or imprinted if you have back problems.
Your rib cage is over your hips.
Eyes gaze forward.
Arms are down by your side.

▶ Exercise:
Inhale to start and exhale as you lift your arms to shoulder height with palms down.
Inhale as you begin pumping your arms from the scapular muscles for five beats and exhale for five beats. One set is five repetitions of inhalation and five of exhalation. Continue till you reach the full Hundred or as many as you are able.

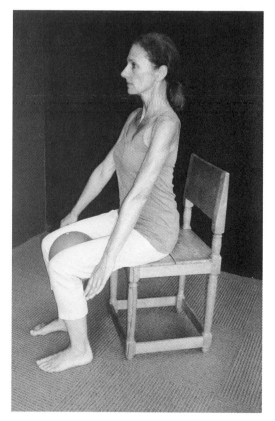

(continued)

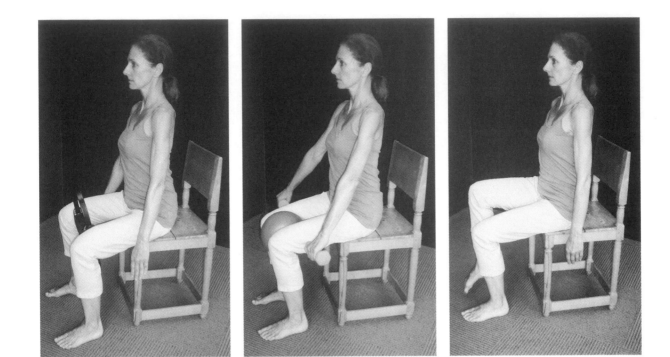

▶ Modifications: For an added challenge:

- Add a Magic Circle between knees.

- Add light hand weights (1–2 pounds). If you are undergoing a breast implant expander program or have undergone TRAM or DIEP flap reconstruction, do not use weights until medically cleared.

- Lift one knee and pump your arms fifty times. Then complete the hundred with your other knee raised.

- Extend one leg and pump your arms fifty times. Then complete the Hundred with your other leg extended.

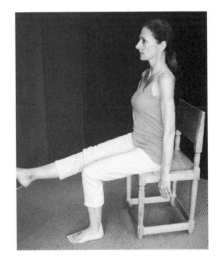

Marching

Goal: To strengthen the abdominals and legs to make walking easier.

Contraindications: None.

Equipment: Chair without arms.

▶ **Start:**

Sit on edge of chair.

Pelvis is in neutral, or imprinted if have back problems.

Your rib cage is over your hips.

Eyes gaze forward.

Arms are down by your side.

▶ **Exercise:**

Inhale to start, then exhale to lift your right knee up just a few inches.

Inhale to place foot on floor, then exhale as you lift your left leg.

Alternate legs to simulate marching.

▶ **Be sure to:**

Using your abdominals, keep pelvis as stable as possible without rocking from side to side or forward and backward.

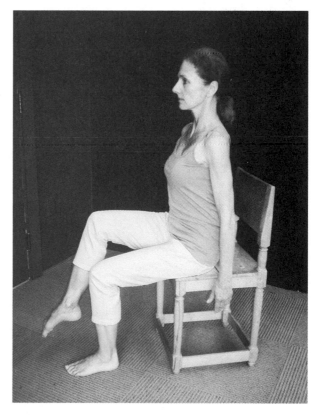

Arm Series: Hug a Tree

Goal: Perform any two of the four exercises in the Arm series. Hug a Tree stretches the chest while strengthening the middle back muscles.

Contraindications: If you are undergoing a breast implant expander program you may need to omit this exercise. Check with your surgeon.

Equipment: Chair without arms.

Medium-sized ball (optional; squeezing the ball between your knees will help to activate the pelvic floor and transverse abdominis muscles and prevent your knees from collapsing in).

▶ Start:

Sit on edge of chair.

Pelvis is in neutral, or imprinted if you have back problems.

Your rib cage is over your hips.

Eyes gaze forward.

Arms are extended in a "T" position, with soft elbows.

Palms face forward.

▶ Exercise:

Inhale to start, then exhale as you bring your arms together as if you are hugging a big oak tree.

Inhale as you hold.

Exhale to return to start.

▶ Be sure to:

Move from the scapular muscles on your back. There should be very little arm movement with this exercise.

▶ Modification: For an added challenge:

• Add light hand weights (1–2 pounds). If you are undergoing a breast implant expander program or have undergone TRAM or DIEP flap reconstruction, do not use weights until medically cleared.

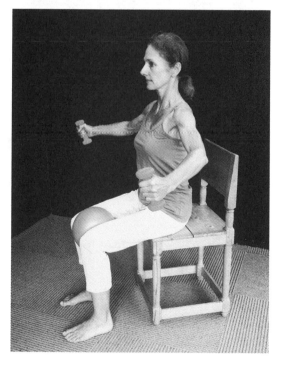

> The focus on proper shoulder girdle biomechanics and middle back strengthening helped counteract the protective posture I tended to use to shield my chest.
>
> —*Beth Mast*

Arm Series: Scissors

Goal: Perform any two of the four exercises in the Arm series. Scissors stretches the sides of your body and underarm area, including the latissimus dorsi, to prepare you for washing windows and taking off clothing such as jackets or hats

Contraindications: If you are undergoing a breast implant expander program this exercise may not be appropriate. Please check with your medical provider.

Equipment: Chair without arms.
Medium-sized ball (optional; squeezing the ball between your knees will help to activate the pelvic floor and transverse abdominis muscles and prevent your knees from collapsing in).

▶ **Start:**
Sit on edge of chair.
Pelvis is in neutral, or imprinted if have back problems.
Your rib cage is over your hips.
Eyes gaze forward.
Arms are extended out in front at shoulder height, with palms facing one another.

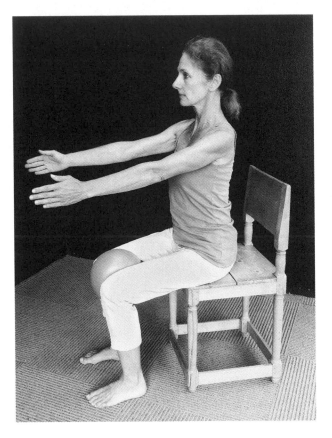

▶ **Exercise:**

Inhale to start, then exhale as you raise your right arm up toward the ceiling and your left arm toward the floor in a scissor motion.

Inhale as you bring both arms back to center.

Exhale as you lift your left arm toward the ceiling and your right arm toward the floor.

Inhale as your arms return to center.

▶ **Modification: For an added challenge:**

• Add light hand weights (1–2 pounds). If you are undergoing a breast implant expander program, or have undergone TRAM or DIEP flap reconstruction, do not use weights until medically cleared.

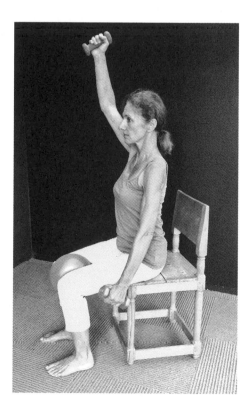

Arm Series: Open the Door

Goal: Perform any two of the four exercises in the Arm series. Open the Door improves strength of the rotator cuff muscles located at the back of the shoulder as well as improving posture. These muscles are very important for shoulder function.

Contraindications: None.

Equipment: Chair without arms.
Medium-sized ball (optional; squeezing the ball between your knees will help to activate the pelvic floor and transverse abdominis muscles and prevent your knees from collapsing in).

▶ Start:

Sit on edge of chair.

Pelvis is in neutral, or imprinted if you have back problems.

Your rib cage is over your hips.

Eyes gaze forward.

Elbows are bent at a 90° angle and glued to your waist.

Palms face each other with thumbs up.

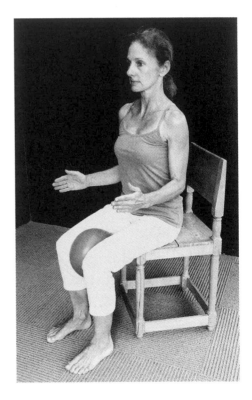

▶ **Exercise:**

Inhale to start, then exhale as you move both arms out to the side while elbows remain glued to your waist.

Inhale as you hold.

Exhale to return to start position.

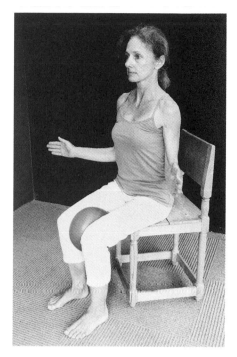

▶ **Modification: For an added challenge:**

- Add light hand weights (1–2 pounds) or a light resistance band. If you are undergoing a breast implant expander program or have undergone TRAM or DIEP flap reconstruction, do not use weights or resistance bands until medically cleared.

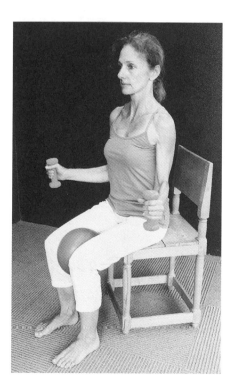
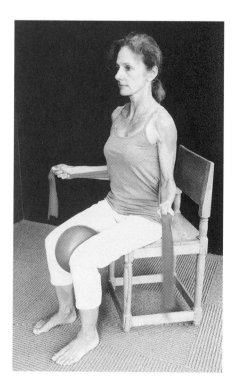

Arm Series: Up "W"

Goal: Perform any two of the four exercises in the Arm series. Up"W"stretches the chest muscles, strengthens the back muscles, and promotes good posture.

Contraindications: If you are undergoing a breast implant expander program or have undergone TRAM or DIEP flap reconstruction, keep shoulders at 90° (shoulder height), not above, and do not use a resistance band until medically cleared.

Equipment: Chair without arms.
Medium-sized ball (optional; squeezing the ball between your knees will help to activate the pelvic floor and transverse abdominis muscles and prevent your knees from collapsing in).

▶ **Start:**
Sit on edge of chair.
Pelvis is in neutral, or imprinted if you have back problems.
Your rib cage is over your hips.
Eyes gaze forward.
Both arms are lifted to shoulder height and bent at the elbows with palms facing out in a "W" or goalpost position.

▶ **Exercise:**
Inhale to start, then exhale as you lift both arms up toward the ceiling.
Inhale as you hold.
Exhale as you bring both arms back to start.

▶ **Modification:**

- Keep arms in a pain free goalpost position as you try and open up the chest musculature, breathing deeply as you stretch arms toward your back.

For an added challenge:

- Use a resistance band.

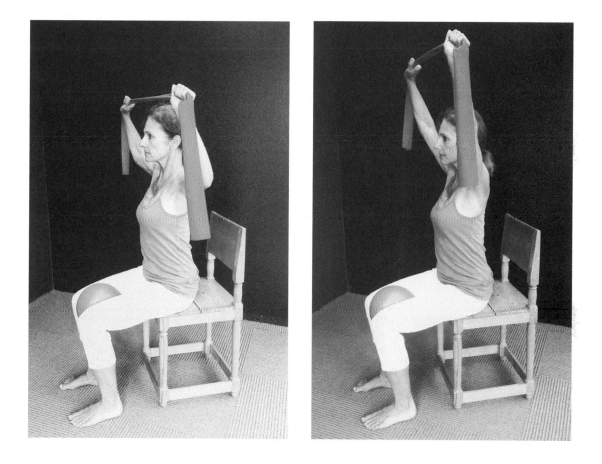

Gaining back strength and flexibility added to my confidence and helped me to feel better emotionally.

—*Grace T.*

Heel Slides

Goal: To learn how to activate and strengthen the core while seated.

Contraindications: None.

Equipment: Chair without arms.
Wear socks or place a towel under your foot.

▶ Start:

Sit on edge of chair.

Pelvis is in neutral, or imprinted if you have back problems.

Your rib cage is over your hips.

Eyes gaze forward.

Arms are down by your side.

▶ Exercise:

Inhale to start and exhale to push the right heel away.

Keep your pelvis level.

Inhale as you hold.

Exhale as you return heel to start position.

Perform five to eight repetitions on the right leg, then switch to the left leg.

▶ Modification:

You can perform this exercise with fewer breaths if you just exhale as you push your heel away and inhale as you bring it back in.

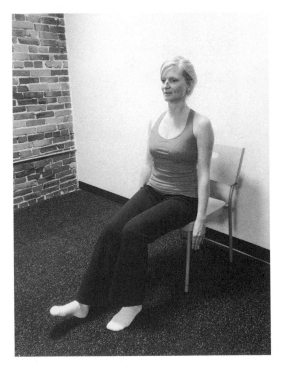

Phase 3

Regaining Strength, Power, and Endurance

If you haven't tried the modifications to add light hand weights suggested for these exercises in Phases 1 and 2, try them now.

- Scapula Protraction and Retraction

- Hundred

- Hug a Tree

- Open the Door

Start with a light weight (1–2 pounds) and see how your body responds. Remember to keep your wrists straight when holding weights.

If you have lymphedema, or are at risk, progress slowly when using weights and do not increase the number of repetitions at the same time as you increase the weights. Be sure to monitor your arm(s) for any symptoms of lymphedema. If you feel heaviness or tightness than the progression may have been too rapid. Be sure to wear your sleeve and gauntlet as recommended by your therapist.

If you are undergoing a breast implant expander program or have undergone TRAM or DIEP flap reconstruction, do not use weights or resistance bands until cleared by your doctor, and eliminate or modify exercises as indicated.

Marching with Arm Lifts

Goal: To strengthen leg, back, and shoulder muscles while building the endurance necessary to perform home and work tasks.

Contraindications: If you are undergoing a breast implant expander program or have undergone TRAM or DIEP flap reconstruction, eliminate the weights.

Equipment: Chair without arms.
Light hand weights (1–2 pounds).

▶ Start:

Sit on edge of chair.

Pelvis is in neutral, or imprinted if you have back problems.

Your rib cage is over your hips.

Eyes gaze forward.

Arms are down by your side with hands holding weights.

▶ Exercise:

Inhale to start, then exhale as you lift your right knee up and both arms out to shoulder height at your sides. Inhale as you drop the right knee and arms toward the chair.

Exhale as you lift your left leg up and both arms out to shoulder height at your sides.

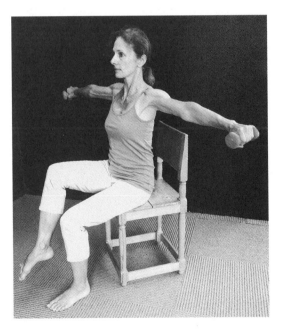

▶ Be sure to:

Keep hips stable and do not rock forward and backward or side to side.

▶ **Modification: To lessen the intensity:**

- Eliminate weights.

Marching with Arm Scissors

Goal: To strengthen shoulders, build endurance, and challenge your coordination.

Contraindications: If you are undergoing a breast implant expander program or have undergone TRAM or DIEP flap reconstruction, eliminate the weights until medically cleared.

Equipment: Chair without arms.
Light hand weights (1–2 pounds).
Stopwatch or timer on phone.

▶ **Start:**

Sit on edge of chair with spine and pelvis in neutral, or imprinted if you have back problems.
Your rib cage is over your hips.
Eyes gaze forward.
Both arms are extended to the front at shoulder height with palms facing one another and hands holding weights.

▶ **Exercise:**

Begin by lifting your right and then your left leg in a marching pattern for 30 seconds.

Continue marching as you inhale, then exhale to bring your right arm toward your head and your left arm down by your side.

Inhale as you bring both arms back to center.

Exhale to bring the left arm up toward your head and the right arm down by your side.

▶ **Modification: To lessen the intensity:**

- Eliminate weights.

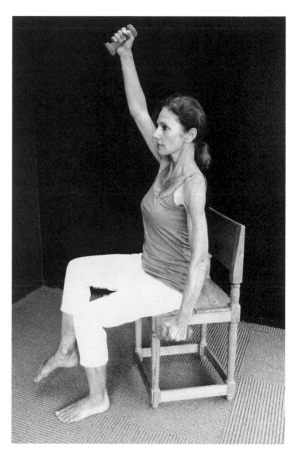

I believe strongly that being active and exercising regularly are the keys to quicker recovery from surgery. While energy levels are severely affected by chemotherapy, the best thing I did for myself was to exercise.

—Bonnie O.

Rowing with Band

Goal: To strengthen back stabilization muscles, including the middle trapezius and rhomboids, and stretch the chest muscles

Contraindications: If you are undergoing a breast implant expander program or have undergone TRAM or DIEP flap reconstruction, eliminate the band until medically cleared; just bring arms to the back as you stretch your chest.

Equipment: Chair without arms.
Resistance band.

▶ Start:

Sit on edge of chair.
Pelvis is in neutral, or imprinted if have back problems.
Your rib cage is over your hips.
Eyes gaze forward.
Place the band in front of your knees and hold the ends in each hand.

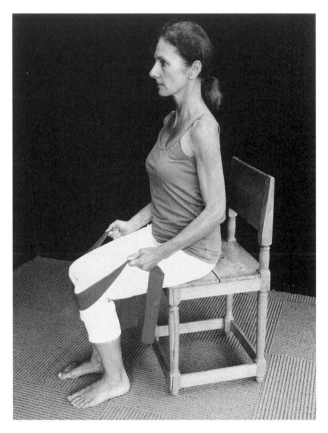

▶ **Exercise:**

Inhale to start and exhale as you pull both arms back, drawing your shoulder blades together on your back and stretching the resistance band.

Return to start position.

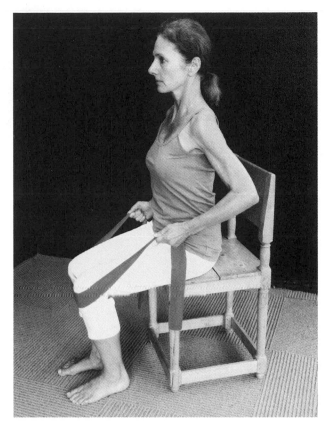

▶ **Modification: To lessen the intensity:**

• Eliminate resistance band.

PART VI

Standing Pilates Program

Standing Pilates challenges your balance and is a weight-bearing form of exercise. Many breast cancer survivors are at risk for osteoporosis. Building bone density and learning to keep your balance are essential when you are at risk for falls, especially as we age. Try to do this program at least a few times a week.

Start by holding onto the wall, a sturdy chair, or a piece of furniture so that you always have something to hold on to if you lose your balance. As your balance improves, you may no longer need a stability base nearby. This is a more advanced program and a goal to work toward.

If you have peripheral neuropathy in your feet, these exercises are not advised. Please perform the chair Pilates program exercises for safety until the peripheral neuropathy is resolved.

If you are at risk for lymphedema, wear a sleeve and gauntlet (glove) if recommended by your health care professional. Progress slowly when using weights and do not increase the number of repetitions at the same time that you increase the weights. Start with a light weight (1–2 pounds).

If you are undergoing a breast implant expander program or have undergone transverse rectus abdominal muscle (TRAM) or deep inferior epigastric perforators (DIEP) flap reconstruction, do not use weights or resistance bands until cleared by your doctor, and eliminate or modify exercises as indicated.

If you have back issues, always use an imprinted spine, not a neutral spine, for all exercises.

If you are undergoing chemotherapy, adhere to your physician's recommendations and precautions.

Phase 1: Protective Phase

With medical clearance, these exercises are safe to do postsurgery with drains in place and can be continued after your drains are removed. Do three to five repetitions of each of these exercises, on each side of the body. This phase will last approximately two to four weeks, or until you feel comfortable progressing to more difficult exercises. The exercises should feel easier and there should be no discomfort before moving on to the next phase. The exercises should be done in the order as presented to establish a daily routine. When you move on to Phase 2 and Phase 3, use the exercises in Phase 1 as your warm-up.

- Pelvic Tilts : Neutral and Imprinted

- Breathing
- Marching in Place
- Scapula Elevation and Depression
- Scapula Protraction and Retraction
- Squats

Phase 2: Return to Function

Once you are comfortable with the Phase 1 exercises, add the exercises in Phase 2 to your routine for two to four weeks. Begin with three to five repetitions of each exercise, gradually increasing to five to eight.

- Footwork Squats:

    Heels Together, Toes Apart

    Toes Turned Out

- Heel Raises: Parallel Position
- Marching with Arms Series:

    Side Lifts

    Scissors

- Hundred

Phase 3: Regaining Strength, Power, and Endurance

Once you are able to do the exercises in Phases 1 and 2 without pain or discomfort, add the following to your routine (approximately 6–8 weeks postsurgery). Begin with three to five repetitions of each exercise, gradually increasing to five to eight.

- Rowing with Band
- Hundred with Lifted Leg

- Single Leg Kick

- Leg Circles

For all exercises, a maximum of five to eight repetitions is recommended. However, everyone is different and you should work within your own tolerance. How you feel can vary from day to day, so please be gentle with yourself.

Please remember to:

- Stretch before and after Pilates or take a warm shower to warm up the body.

- Always alternate arm and leg exercises to prevent fatigue, and rest when needed.

- Drink plenty of water to stay hydrated.

What Is Good Standing Posture?

Questions to ask yourself:

- Are my feet hip distance apart?

- Are my feet and legs directly under my hips?

- Are my feet parallel and my weight balanced through the middle of each foot?

- Is my weight on my big and little toes as well as my heels? Are my knees lined up and parallel with my hip bones?

- Is my pelvis in a neutral position so that my back is not arched forward or too far back, or is it imprinted because of back problems?

- Is my rib cage over my hips?

- Are my shoulders under my ears?

- Are my shoulders level and neutral, not lifted up to my ears with my shoulder blades down my back?

- Are my arms facing down with palms toward my body?

- Is my chest open?

- Is my gaze forward with my throat open and chin resting naturally?

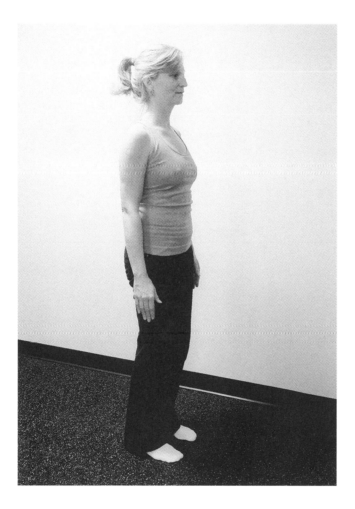

Phase 1

Protective Phase

Pelvic Tilts: Neutral and Imprinted

Goal: To learn the neutral and imprinted position when standing, which can be difficult at first.

Contraindications: If you have peripheral neuropathy, this exercise is not advised.

Equipment: Wall.

▶ **Start:**

Stand with your back 6 to 12 inches away from the wall, with feet hip distance apart and knees slightly bent.

Shoulder blades and head are touching the wall.

Your rib cage is over your hips.

Shoulders are relaxed and hands placed with your ring and little fingers on your hip bones and your index fingers and thumbs touching to form a heart around your belly button. Hands are perpendicular to the floor.

Eyes gaze forward.

▶ **Exercise:**

Inhale to start and exhale as you tilt your pelvis toward the wall (imprint). Your index fingers will now be further forward than your thumbs.

Inhale as you hold.

Exhale as you return your pelvis to neutral with both thumbs and fingers on the same plane.

▶ **Be sure to:**

Keep both knees bent if necessary to imprint, and keep shoulder blades and head against the wall.

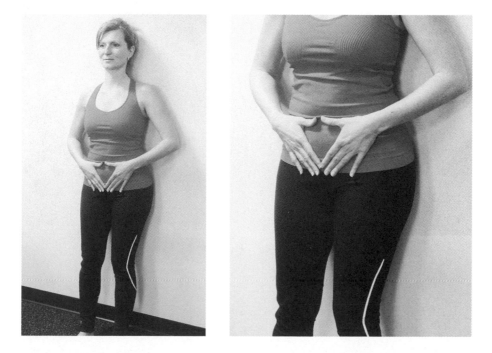

Breathing

Goal: To learn the Pilates method of rib cage breathing while standing.

Contraindications: If you have peripheral neuropathy, this exercise is not advised.

Equipment: None.

▶ Start:

Stand facing forward with feet hip distance apart.

Pelvis is in neutral, or imprinted if you have back problems.

Your rib cage is over your hips.

Shoulders are relaxed, with hands resting over your rib cage.

Eyes gaze forward.

▶ Exercise:

Place fingers by sides and front of your rib cage.

Inhale to "smell the roses" as you feel your rib cage expand to the front, side, and back.

Exhale to "blow out the candles" as you feel your rib cage grow smaller.

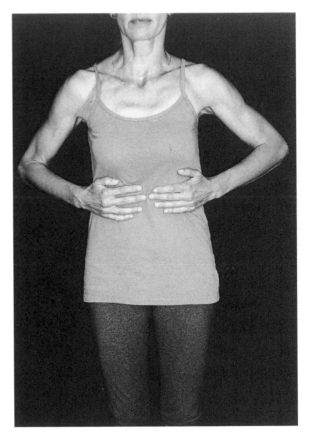

Marching in Place

Goal: To warm up the body and increase blood flow to your arms and legs while building balance, endurance, and strength.

Contraindications: If you have peripheral neuropathy, this exercise is not advised.
If drains are still in place, this exercise may be difficult for you. Keep knees low and perform gentle marching.

Equipment: Timer or stopwatch.

▶ Start:

Stand facing forward with feet hip distance apart.
Pelvis is in neutral, or imprinted if you have back problems.
Your rib cage is over your hips.
Arms are down by your sides with shoulders relaxed.
Eyes gaze forward.
Set timer or stopwatch for 30 seconds.

▶ Exercise:

Begin marching in place by lifting your knees as high as you can without bending forward. Continue marching for 30 seconds.
Increase the amount of time that you spend marching by 30-second intervals each week. This will help build your aerobic endurance.

▶ Be sure to:

Keep back straight. Do not arch or bend your back.

(*continued*)

▶ **Modification: To increase the intensity:**

- Add pumping your arms.

Scapula Elevation and Depression

Goal: To improve scapular mobility in preparation for shoulder movement.

Contraindications: If you have peripheral neuropathy, this exercise is not advised.

Equipment: Wall.

▶ **Start:**

Stand with your back leaning against the wall, with feet 6 to 12 inches away from wall and hip distance apart. Knees are slightly bent.

Shoulder blades and head are touching the wall.

Pelvis is in neutral (there may be space between the wall and lower back), or imprinted if you have back problems.

Your rib cage is over your hips.

Arms are down by your sides and shoulders are relaxed.

Eyes gaze forward.

▶ **Exercise:**

Inhale as you elevate shoulders to the ears.

Exhale as you reach fingertips to the floor by bringing your shoulder muscles down.

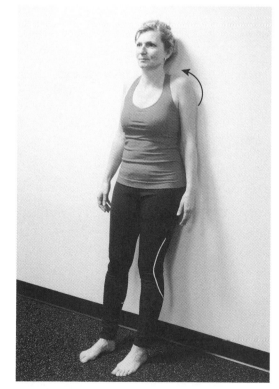

Elevation

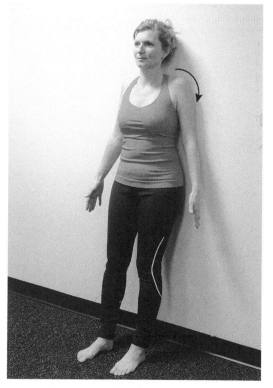

Depression

Scapula Protraction and Retraction

Goal: To activate and strengthen the scapular muscles that are integral to proper shoulder function.

Contraindications: If you have peripheral neuropathy, this exercise is not advised.

Equipment: Wall.

▶ Start:

Stand with your back leaning against the wall, with feet 6 to 12 inches away from wall and hip distance apart. Knees are slightly bent.

Pelvis is in neutral, or imprinted if you have back problems.

Your rib cage is over your hips.

Shoulders are relaxed and arms raised to shoulder height or within your comfort zone.

Eyes gaze forward.

▶ Exercise:

Inhale as you reach forward as if "hugging a child." Your shoulder blades should come off the wall. This is protraction.

Exhale as you bring your shoulder blades together (imagine lightly squeezing a tiny ball placed between your shoulder blades). You will feel your shoulder blades against the wall. This is retraction.

Protraction

Retraction

▶ Modification: For an added challenge:

- Place a large therapy ball on the wall behind your middle to lower back. You will need to move your feet further forward.

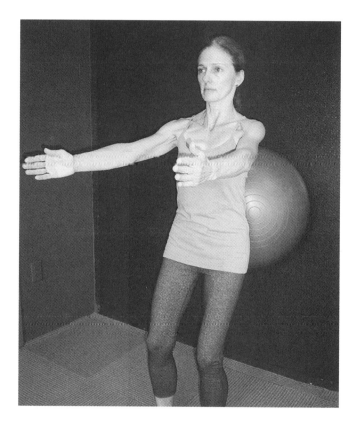

Squats

Goal: To increase strength of your quadriceps, improving your ability to walk and climb stairs.

Contraindications: If you have peripheral neuropathy, this exercise is not advised.
If you have any knee problems, only bend to a non-painful position or eliminate this exercise.

Equipment: Wall.

▶ Start:

Stand with your back leaning against the wall, with feet 6 to 12 inches away from wall (or more if comfortable) and hip distance apart.

Shoulder blades and head are touching the wall.

Pelvis is in neutral, or imprinted if you have back problems.

Your rib cage is over your hips.

Arms are down by your sides and shoulders are relaxed.

Eyes gaze forward.

▶ Exercise:

Inhale to start, then exhale as you bend both knees to a 90° angle. You will feel your back sliding down the wall and your weight mostly on your heels.

Inhale as you return to start position.

▶ Be sure to:

Keep shoulder blades and head on wall and weight on heels. Keep pelvis in the same position as when you started.

▶ **Modifications: For an added challenge:**

- Place a large therapy ball on the wall behind your middle to lower back.
- Hold your knees in the bent position for 5 to 10 seconds before you come up.

Phase 2

Return to Function

Footwork Squats: Heels Together, Toes Apart

Goal: In Pilates and ballet, this would be referred to as a first position. To strengthen your inner thighs and help to connect you to your core and pelvic floor.

Contraindications: If you have peripheral neuropathy, this exercise is not advised.

Equipment: Wall.

▶ Start:

Stand with your back leaning against the wall, with feet 6 to 12 inches away from wall and hip distance apart. Heels are together and toes apart.

Shoulder blades and head are touching the wall.

Pelvis is in neutral, or imprinted if you have back problems.

Your rib cage is over your hips.

Arms are down by your sides and shoulders are relaxed.

Eyes gaze forward.

▶ Exercise:

Inhale to start, then exhale as you bend your knees while keeping the heels together and anchored to the floor.

Inhale to return to the start position. Imagine zipping up your inner thighs as you come up.

You will feel your back sliding down and up as you perform this exercise.

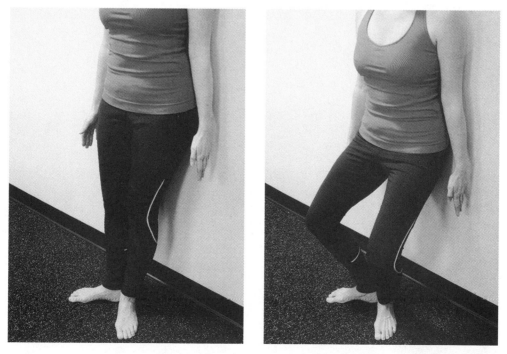

(continued)

▶ **Modifications:**

Keep the knee bends small if you have tight calves.

For an added challenge:

- Place a large therapy ball on the wall behind your middle to lower back.

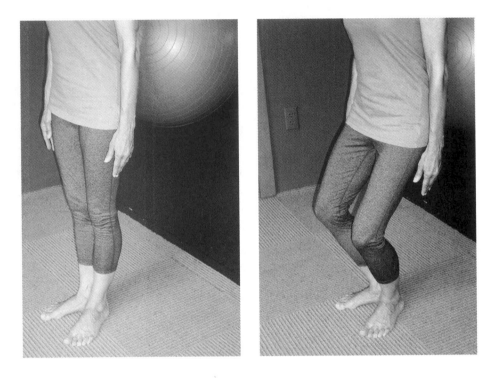

Footwork Squats: Toes Turned Out

Goal: In Pilates and ballet, this would be referred to as a second position. This exercise helps you to keep your pelvis as still as possible while moving the legs and strengthens the quadriceps and hamstrings.

Contraindications: If you have peripheral neuropathy, this exercise is not advised.

Equipment: Wall.

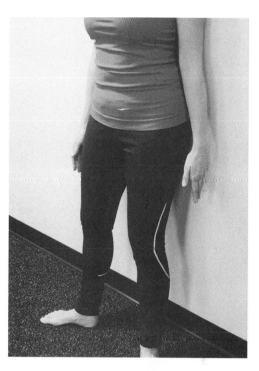

▶ Start:

Stand with your back to the wall, feet are 6 to 12 inches away from the wall and hip distance apart. Thighs are turned out so knees and feet are facing away from each other.

Shoulder blades and head are touching the wall.

Pelvis is in neutral, or imprinted if you have back problems. Your rib cage is over your hips.

Arms are down by your sides and shoulders are relaxed. Eyes gaze forward.

▶ Exercise:

Inhale to start and exhale as you bend your knees, making sure to track knees over toes; knees should not go past the toes.

Inhale and return to start.

You will feel your back sliding down and up the wall as you move.

▶ Be sure to:

Keep heels on the ground.

(continued)

▶ Modification: For an added challenge:

- Place a therapy ball on the wall behind your middle to lower back.

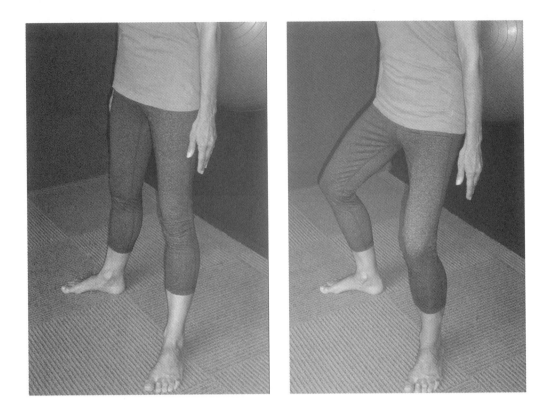

Heel Raises: Parallel Position

Goal: To improve balance and strengthen ankles for walking and climbing stairs.

Contraindications: If you have peripheral neuropathy, this exercise is not advised.

Equipment: Wall.

▶ Start:

Stand with your back to the wall, feet are 6 to 12 inches away from the wall and hip distance apart, in parallel, with toes forward.

Shoulder blades and head are touching the wall.

Pelvis is in neutral, or imprinted if you have back problems.

Your rib cage is over your hips.

Arms are down by your sides and shoulders are relaxed.

Eyes gaze forward.

▶ Exercise:

Inhale to start, then exhale as you lift both heels off the ground.

Inhale as you hold this position and balance for 5 to 10 seconds. Gradually extend the time period as you feel more comfortable.

Exhale to lower heels and return to start.

You will feel your back sliding up and down the wall.

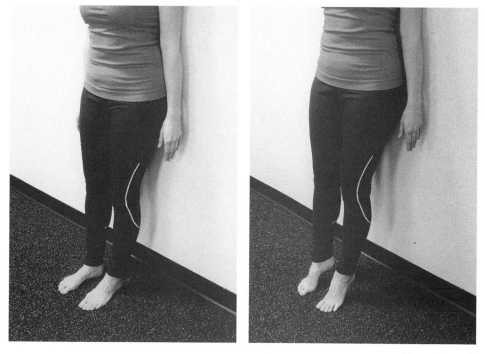

(continued)

▶ **Modifications: For an added challenge:**

- As your balance improves, stand sideways to the wall. Keep one arm within reach of the wall in case you lose your balance.

- Place a therapy ball on the wall behind your middle to lower back.

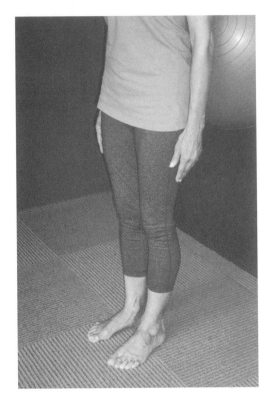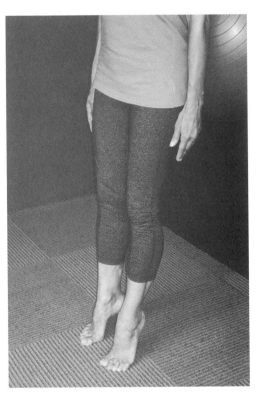

Marching with Arms Series

The purpose of the Marching with Arms series is to increase arm strength while challenging your balance and endurance.

These exercises are more difficult, so be sure to position yourself close to a stable piece of furniture or by the wall.

Do only three to five repetitions of each of these.

Begin by choosing one of these exercises. As you become stronger, gradually incorporate more exercises into your routine.

Always remember to wear your sleeve and gauntlet if recommended by your medical provider.

Marching with Arms: Side Lifts

Goal: To increase balance, endurance, and coordination while stabilizing your pelvis.

Contraindications: If you have peripheral neuropathy, this exercise is not advised.

Equipment: Timer or stopwatch.

▶ **Start:**

Stand with feet hip distance apart, in parallel.

Pelvis is in neutral, or imprinted if you have back problems.

Your rib cage is over your hips.

Arms are down by your sides and shoulders are relaxed.

Eyes gaze forward.

Set timer or stopwatch for 30 seconds.

▶ **Exercise:**

Begin marching in place as you inhale and exhale while keeping your pelvis stable at all times.

Lift knees as high as you can (without bending forward).

Add arms by raising them up to the side in a T position with thumbs up.

March for 30 seconds.

▶ Modifications:

As you become more comfortable, gradually increase the time to one minute and then one minute and 30 seconds.

For an added challenge:

- Add light hand weights (1–2 pounds) while holding weights palm down. If you are undergoing a breast implant expander program or have undergone TRAM or DIEP flap reconstruction, do not use weights until medically cleared.

Marching with Arms: Scissors

Goal: To increase endurance, coordination, and strength.

Contraindications: If you have peripheral neuropathy, this exercise is not advised.

Equipment: Timer or stopwatch.

▶ Start:

Stand with feet hip distance apart, in parallel.

Pelvis is in neutral, or imprinted if you have back problems.

Your rib cage is over your hips.

Arms are down by your sides and shoulders are relaxed.

Eyes gaze forward.

Set timer or stopwatch to 30 seconds.

▶ Exercise:

Begin marching in place while keeping your pelvis neutral, or imprinted if necessary, at all times.

Lift knees as high as you can (without bending forward).

Inhale as you lift your arms to shoulder height in front of you with palms facing each other.

Exhale as you bring your right arm up and your left arm down in a scissor like motion.

Inhale as you return arms to shoulder height.
Exhale to bring the left arm up and the right arm down.
Continue to alternate arms while marching in place.
March for 30 seconds.

▶ Modifications:

As you become more comfortable, gradually increase the time to one minute and then one minute and thirty seconds.

For an added challenge:

- Add light hand weights (1–2 pounds). If you are undergoing a breast implant expander program or have undergone TRAM or DIEP flap reconstruction, do not use weights until medically cleared.

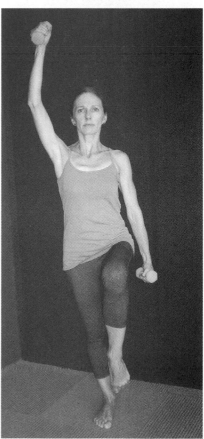

Hundred

Goal: To increase the strength and endurance of the scapular muscles and arms while increasing lung capacity and balance.

Contraindications: If you have peripheral neuropathy, this exercise is not advised.

Equipment: None.

▶ Start:

Stand with feet hip distance apart, in parallel.

Pelvis is in neutral, or imprinted if you have back problems.

Your rib cage is over your hips.

Arms are down by your sides and shoulders are relaxed.

Eyes gaze forward.

▶ Exercise:

Inhale to start, then exhale to lift arms up to a 45° angle or as high as you are able. You may raise your arms as high as shoulder height.

Inhale for five beats while you pump your arms from the scapular muscles (back of shoulders).

Exhale for five beats. This counts as one cycle.

Repeat 10 times until you reach the Hundred or your maximum.

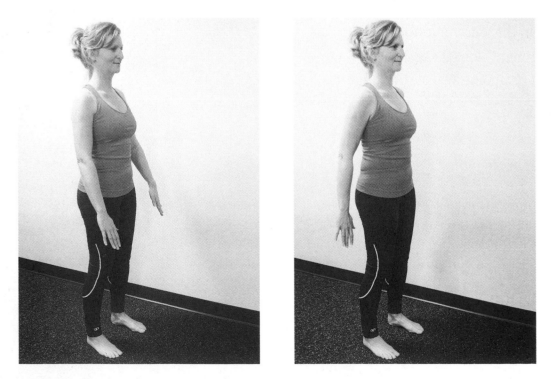

▶ **Modifications:**

Hold chair for support and pump one arm at a time.

For an added challenge:

- March in place as you perform the Hundred.

Phase 3

Regaining Strength, Power, and Endurance

If you haven't tried the modifications to add light hand weights suggested for these exercises in Phase 2, try them now.

- Marching with Arms: Side Lifts

- Marching with Arms: Scissors

Start with light weights (1–2 pounds) and see how your body responds. Remember to keep your wrists straight when holding weights.

If you have lymphedema, or are at risk, progress slowly when using weights and do not increase the number of repetitions at the same time that you increase the weights. Be sure to monitor your arm(s) for any symptoms of lymphedema. If you feel heaviness or tightness the progression may have been too rapid. Be sure to wear your sleeve and gauntlet as recommended by your therapist.

If you are undergoing a breast implant expander program or have undergone TRAM or DIEP flap reconstruction, do not use weights and eliminate or modify exercises as indicated until medically cleared.

Rowing With Band

Goal: To strengthen the muscles in the middle back, promoting good posture as well as shoulder stability.

Contraindication: If you have peripheral neuropathy, this exercise is not advised, but it can be performed while seated.

If you are undergoing a breast implant expander program or have undergone TRAM or DIEP flap reconstruction, eliminate the band. Just pull your arms straight back behind you to stretch the chest and then bring them back.

Equipment: Resistance band.

▶ Start:

Stand with feet hip distance apart, in parallel.

Pelvis is in neutral, or imprinted if you have back problems.

Your rib cage is over your hips.

Eyes gaze forward.

Wrap resistance band around a bedpost or staircase post (anything sturdy that cannot move).

Arms are at your sides, with elbows bent and hands holding each end of band.

▶ Exercise:

Inhale to start, then exhale as you pull the band back while bending elbows.

Inhale and return to start.

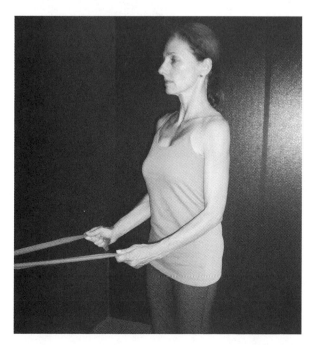 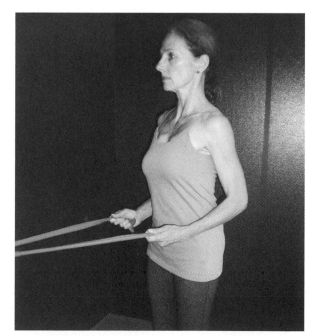

Hundred with Lifted Leg

Goal: To strengthen the entire body, including your arms, abdominal region, and legs, while improving balance.

Contraindications: If you have peripheral neuropathy, this exercise is not advised.

If you are undergoing a breast implant expander program or have undergone TRAM or DIEP flap reconstruction, eliminate the band until medically cleared.

Equipment: Wall.

Resistance band.

▶ Start:

Stand with your back leaning against the wall, with feet 6 to 12 inches away from wall and hip distance apart, in parallel.

Shoulder blades and head are touching the wall.

Pelvis is in neutral, or imprinted if you have back problems.

Your rib cage is over your hips.

Arms are down by your sides and shoulders are relaxed.

Eyes gaze forward.

▶ **Exercise:**

Inhale as you imprint your pelvis against the wall. Exhale as you gently lift your right leg about 2 to 3 inches off the floor.

Inhale and then exhale as you lift your arms up to a 45° angle or shoulder height.

Inhale for five beats while pumping arms from the scapular muscles.

Exhale for five beats untill you reach 50 (five cycles of inhales and exhales) and then switch legs.

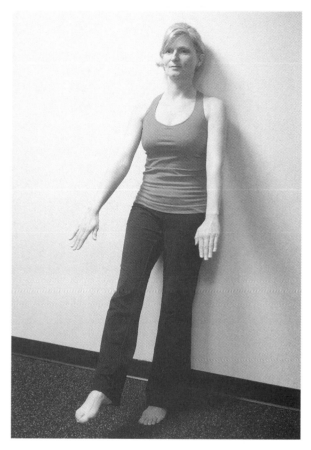

▶ **Modifications:**

For more stability, pump one arm at a time while the other arm holds on to the wall. Eliminate the arms if they easily fatigue.

To lessen the challenge:

- Rest your big toe lightly on the floor.

For an added challenge:

- Move your leg up and down as you move both arms.

Single Leg Kick

Goal: To strengthen the gluteal muscles while challenging your balance.

Contraindications: If you have peripheral neuropathy, this exercise is not advised. This is a very advanced exercise, so proceed with caution.

Equipment: None.

▶ Start:

Stand facing forward with feet hip distance apart and in parallel.

Pelvis is in neutral, or imprinted if you have back problems.

Your rib cage is over your hips.

Arms are down by your sides and shoulders are relaxed.

Eyes gaze forward.

▶ Exercise:

Inhale and exhale as you extend your right leg with foot flexed to the front.

Inhale with a sniffing breath as you kick the right leg from the hip two times to the front.

Exhale as you point your toes and kick once to the back.

This counts as one repetition. Perform five to eight repetitions and then switch legs.

 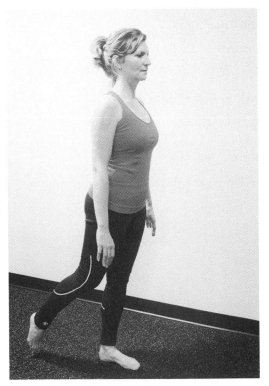

▶ **Modifications:**

Hold onto a wall or chair for support.

For an added challenge:

- Add light hand weights (1–2 pounds). If you are undergoing a breast implant expander program or have undergone TRAM or DIEP flap reconstruction, do not use weights until medically cleared.

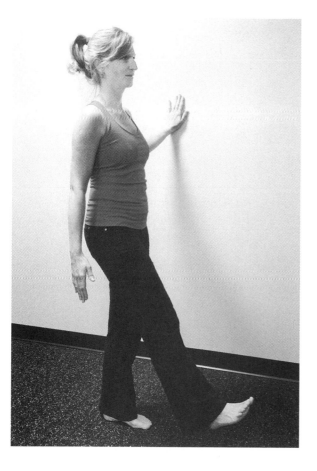
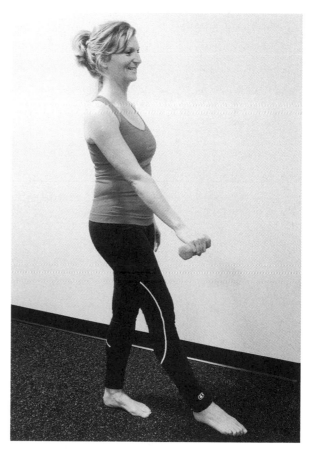

Leg Circles

Goal: To strengthen the adductor and abductor hip muscles that are necessary for walking, and challenge your balance.

Contraindications: If you have peripheral neuropathy, this exercise is not advised.
This is a very challenging exercise, so proceed with caution.

Equipment: None.

▶ **Start:**

Stand facing forward with feet hip distance apart.

Pelvis is in neutral, or imprinted if you have back problems.

Your rib cage is over your hips.

Arms are down by your sides and shoulders are relaxed.

Eyes gaze forward.

▶ **Exercise:**

Inhale and exhale to point toes and extend your right leg out in front of your body.

Inhale and exhale as you circle your right leg clockwise to the side, back, and front. Perform five to eight repetitions.

Inhale and exhale as you extend your right leg in front of your body with your toes pointed. Reverse the circle counterclockwise, to the back, side, and front. Perform five to eight repetitions.

Inhale as you bring your right leg down and switch legs.

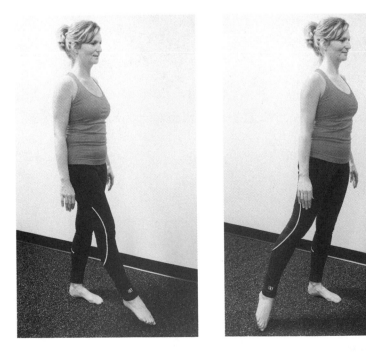

▶ Modifications:

Hold onto a heavy piece of furniture or chair for support.

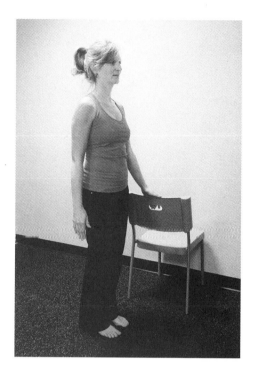

To lessen the intensity:

- Lower height of working leg to toe tap, making circles on the ground.
- Make the circles smaller.

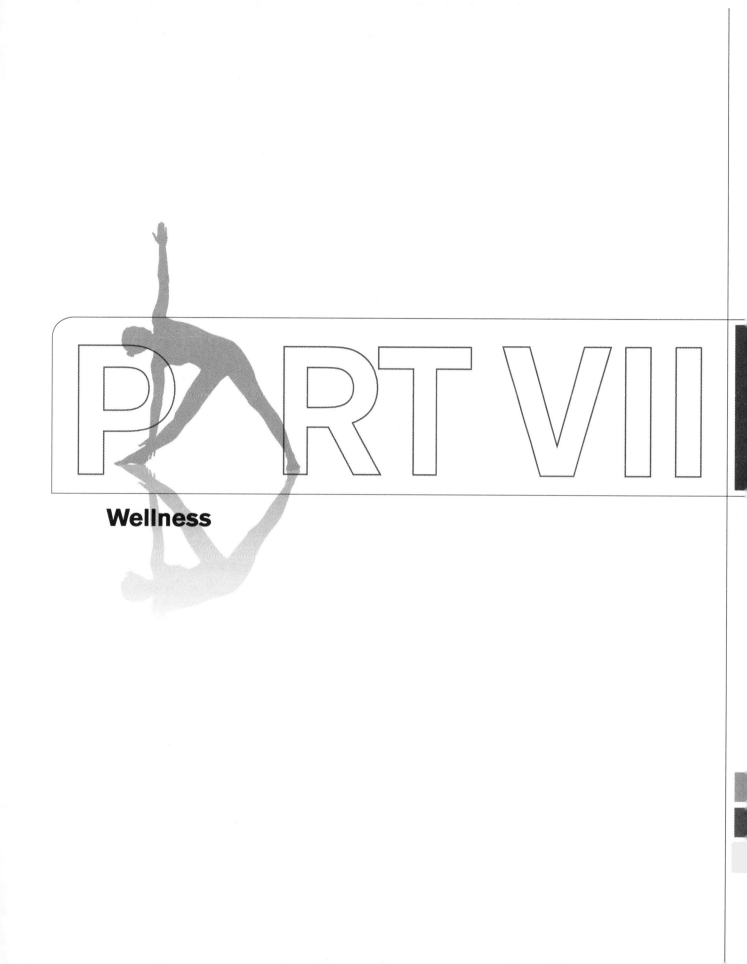

PART VII

Wellness

The information in this section will help improve your quality of life. Even as you become stronger through Pilates practice, there are many lifestyle changes that can help ease the most common side effects of cancer treatment, and a range of equipment is available to assist with your daily tasks. Check the resources section for more information, shops, and organizations that can help as you work toward recovery.

Fatigue

Fatigue is one of the most debilitating aspects of cancer treatment. Cancer-related fatigue is all-encompassing and overwhelming. Once it affects your activities of daily living and ability to perform previously enjoyed leisure activities, quality of life can suffer. Ironically, too much rest and too little activity promotes fatigue.

Learn how to manage your energy and fatigue by planning your day. Prioritize what is really important. Make an energy level or fatigue scale with a 0 to 10 guideline. Zero would be exhaustion and 10 would be high energy. Record your energy levels at different parts of the day—there is usually a pattern. You should tackle your most challenging tasks when your energy level is highest. Many people find their peak energy period is in the morning, but it can be at any point in the day.

Be sure to check with your physician to see if your fatigue can be attributed to a medical issue such as anemia, low thyroid activity, or menopausal symptoms. Show him or her your energy level self-assessment.

Here is some food for thought to work smarter not harder!

- Try and get six to eight hours of good restful sleep.

- If you feel you need rest breaks during your day, find ways to work them into your schedule.

- Take a look at your daily intake of caffeine (all forms, including liquid and food, i.e., chocolate) and gradually decrease that amount.

- Make an appointment with a nutritionist to check that you are getting the appropriate amount of nutrients such as protein in your diet.

- Try to eat five to six smaller meals.

- Drink six to eight glasses of water a day—dehydration can wear you down.

- Are you using good body mechanics to perform tasks? Be sure to lift objects with your knees bent and with both hands, and use a cart to carry heavy objects.

- Use energy conservation techniques such as sitting whenever possible. Set up task areas in the kitchen, where everything needed for a task will be within your reach.

- Is your workstation set up ergonomically? Are you using the proper posture and body mechanics? Recheck your computer and seat height.

- Make exercise a priority—studies have shown that cancer patients who exercise experience less fatigue.

- Take advantage of free services for responsibilities such as house-cleaning or childcare that can be burdensome when undergoing treatment.

Sleep Positioning and Hygiene

Elevating and supporting the affected arm while sleeping or resting will help with shoulder pain and lymphedema. Using a therapeutic memory foam pillow is one alternative for the head and neck to have support while you are sleeping. It is not wise to use more than one pillow under the neck because it brings your neck too far forward, causing neck strain. Instead, try using extra pillows under the arms.

If you are a side sleeper, one option is to lie on your pain-free side with your legs slightly bent. Extend the bottom arm and then bring it in by using both arms to hug a pillow to your chest. You can use a firm pillow between the legs when side sleeping to help your alignment. You do not want your top hip to flop forward and rotate your spine. (The position described will benefit those with back pain too).

Whatever position you choose, be sure to position the shoulder on the pillow so it is not popped forward and remains in line with the neck. The arm should be kept elevated within the position of comfort with the whole arm supported by pillows. Be aware that tucking your bottom arm under the head strains the brachial plexus (the nerves that go down the arm) and should be avoided. You might need to load up on extra pillows for comfort. Investing in a good mattress and pillow is important for optimal sleep hygiene.

Arm Positions for Sleeping

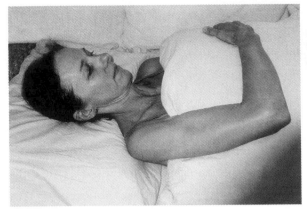 

On your back   **On your side**

Develop a Relaxing Routine Before Bedtime

- Wear cotton or other natural fibers to sleep in.

- Try to go to bed at the same time every night and wake up at the same time every morning. Changing these times on the weekends is not conducive to restful regular sleep. Nap only 15 to 20 minutes in the early afternoon.

- Take a warm bath with lavender essential oil 90 to 120 minutes before sleep.

- Listen to relaxation or sleep CDs.

- Have a cup of warm milk with honey or chamomile tea 30 minutes to an hour before bedtime.

- Apply warm sesame oil to the bottom of your feet.

- If you don't fall asleep within 30 minutes of getting into bed, leave bed and do something relaxing, such as reading a book, in another room.

Bedroom

- The bedroom should be used for two activities: sleeping and sex.

- Remove all electronic devices (cell phones, computers, digital clocks, and televisions) from your bedroom. LED lighting tells the brain to stay awake.

- Remove unwanted clutter from the bedroom to create a sense of calm rather than chaos.

- Create complete darkness in the bedroom by adding window treatments such as blackout curtains.

- Sound machines with white noise can help you relax.

- Consider wearing earplugs if there is unavoidable noise.

- The room temperature should be cool and comfortable. An overly warm environment is not conducive to sleeping—lower the temperature in the house or bedroom before going to sleep.

Foods and Liquids

- Avoid caffeine, chocolate, colas, or other stimulants within one hour of bedtime.

- Alcohol can cause a rebound effect, initially making you sleepy then waking you several hours later. It is best to avoid drinking before going to sleep.

- Avoid eating a heavy dinner within two to three hours of bedtime.

- Avoid drinking a lot of fluids within two hours of bedtime so that bathroom trips can be avoided.

Exercise

- Daily aerobic exercise such as walking or cycling energizes you. This can help combat treatment fatigue and help you sleep better. It is best done earlier in the day, five to six hours before bedtime.

- Exercise such as Pilates and yoga can help relax the body and calm the mind.

Lymphedema: Daily Living Recommendations (with Mary Essert, BA)

Outdoors

- Protect the affected arm from sunburn by wearing sunscreen outdoors.

- Avoid insect bites by wearing insect repellant.

- Wear gloves when gardening.

- Avoid repetitive movements such as pruning shrubs, and be careful around plants that "bite."

Indoors

- Wear gloves when doing housework.

- Use mitts when moving hot items from the oven.

- Use both hands to lift while bending at the knees. Slide objects when possible. Use carts to carry heavy items such as groceries, and use suitcases on wheels.

- Avoid sustained activities such as painting unless you have properly prepared for this activity by warming up your neck and shoulders. Wear your compression garments if applicable.

- Use your sleeve and gauntlet when you must lift heavy objects or when performing repetitive tasks such as vacuuming.

Daily Living

- Keep arm as cool as possible.

- Elevate arm with a pillow when sleeping.

- Keep arm clean, supple, and well moisturized.

- Use warm, not hot, water when bathing.

- Wear loose clothing, jewelry, and watches.

- Use a backpack to carry any necessary items so the weight can be evenly distributed rather than on one shoulder.

- Wear a sleeve and gauntlet if recommended by your medical provider.

- Do not cut cuticles.

- Avoid temperature extremes, whether cold or hot (hot tubs or saunas).

Medical

- Alert all health professionals to use the unaffected arm when withdrawing blood, taking blood pressure, or giving vaccinations or other shots. If you have had a double mastectomy, avoid these same procedures being done on the arm where lymph nodes were removed.

Travel

- The National Lymphedema Network recommends that individuals with a confirmed diagnosis of lymphedema should wear some form of compression therapy when traveling by air. If you are at risk, you should check with your medical provider.

- Use suitcases on wheels.

- Ask for assistance when lifting your luggage or placing it in overhead bins.

Chemo Brain: Memory Boosters and Helpful Hints

Chemo brain has been described as changes in memory, concentration, and attention and loss of the ability to perform different mental tasks after undergoing chemotherapy. You may have trouble concentrating, learning new tasks, remembering names or common words, or multitasking, and may feel that you are thinking slower.

Get Organized

- Do one thing at a time. Don't multitask.

- Establish specific places to keep your keys, wallet, and cell phone. For example, place keys near the front door daily.

- Use a detailed calendar or organizer to keep track of appointments. Hang it in a prominent place such as on the refrigerator and mark all important dates on it and/or on your smartphone.

- Leave reminder messages on your smartphone.

- Make lists. Keep a pad in your pocketbook to write down everything that needs to be remembered, and keep sticky notes around the house. Use calendar alerts on your smartphone.

- Color code or label cabinets or drawers where you store things that you use frequently.

- Keep important phone numbers easily displayed next to the phone or in your contact list.

- Keep your home as free of clutter as possible.

- Prepare for tomorrow. Make your lunch at night and take out clothing that you will wear for the next day to avoid rushing.

- If it's OK with your doctor, bring someone with you to your doctors' appointments to write down the information.

- Keep a binder of your test results so that they are easily accessible.

- Buy folders and keep medical records stored by month and year.

- Make a clearly labeled folder to keep your bills organized.

- Repeat directions out loud or to yourself.

- Take a mental picture of where your car is parked or, even better, take an actual photo with your smartphone.

- Keep track of your changes in memory by keeping a diary.

Brain Exercises

- Do puzzles like Sudoku, crossword, or word searches. Here are some websites that offer free programs or free trials: www.fitbrains.com, www.luminosity.com, and www.memory-improvement-tips.com.

- Learn something new, such as a language, activity, or craft that stimulates your brain.

- Use wordplay such as rhyming to remember peoples' names. For example, repeat to yourself, "I have to put this salad back into the refrigerator." Salad should help you with the name Sala.

Stay Healthy

- Eat a healthy diet.

- Exercise daily. Staying physically active will stimulate blood flow.

- Pilates can help you to relax and regain some clarity.

- Get plenty of rest.

Peripheral Neuropathy

Chemotherapy-induced peripheral neuropathy (CIPN) is related to some of the chemotherapy drugs such as Taxol. You may experience weakness, burning, numbness, and tingling in your feet and/or hands. Sometimes these side effects can resolve quickly but they may last longer. Some of these suggestions may also be helpful after breast reconstruction surgery, since it can be difficult to bend down after this procedure.

Dressing

- Wear supportive footwear such as sneakers or sturdy shoes with closed back and toes, insoles, and nonskid soles. Eliminate heels.

- Use Velcro on sneakers and clothing.

- Use built-up, adaptive dressing equipment such as button hooks and zipper pulls if necessary. See an occupational therapist for more recommendations.

- Use stocking aides and long-handled shoehorns for putting on socks and shoes.

- Avoid ill-fitting footwear. Regularly check for proper fit. Blisters and injuries are indications that your shoes are too tight.

- Avoid ill-fitting clothes as they may exacerbate CIPN.

Daily Living

- Use gloves when washing dishes, working outdoors, or doing home repairs.

- Use potholders or mitts with hot and cold items.

- Secure or remove throw rugs.

- Make sure that there is adequate lighting, and use nightlights for safety when waking up at night.

- Place bathmats and install grab bars by tub.

- Use the handrails when negotiating stairs.

- Keep hands and feet well covered and warm with gloves, socks, and boots.

Workstation

- Use voice activated software for computers and electronic devices.

- Use built-up handles or grippers on pencils and pens for better grasp, and Dycem under paper. (Dycem is a nonslip plastic material used to provide extra traction to everyday objects. It is sold in rolls and can be cut to appropriate sizes.)

- Sit whenever possible to perform station tasks, and keep all necessary items close.

Hygiene

- Test water temperature with arm and set hot water heater to within 105° F to 120° F to prevent burns. Use a handheld shower hose.

- Use foam tubing to make handles on toothbrush, hair brush, comb, or makeup brushes easier to grip. You can purchase foam through therapy catalogs.

- Use liquid bath gels instead of a bar of soap.

- Keep a bath mat in the shower or get a shower seat or bench for safety.

- Keep feet clean and dry.

Pain

- Learn strategies to control pain, such as biofeedback or breathing techniques.

- Massage hands and feet daily.

- If hands are painful when touching items, use paper tape at the fingertips.

- Get a referral to an occupational therapist or physical therapist for TENS (transcutaneous electrical nerve stimulation, a machine that can help with pain by providing mild electric impulses).

Glossary

ADL—Activities of Daily Living. Daily tasks such as dressing, bathing, and feeding.

Autonomic Nervous System—The part of the nervous system that is concerned with involuntary bodily functions such as sweating, rising blood pressure, or gooseflesh. Otherwise known as "fight or flight" when involved in emergency situations.

Axilla (Axillary region)—Under the arm or armpit area, where lymph nodes are removed. This area can be painful after surgery.

Core—In Pilates, the core refers to the diaphragm, multifidus, transverse abdominis, and pelvic floor.

Energy Conservation Techniques—Modifications of daily tasks that can help you when you are fatigued.

Extension—The movement of the limb into the straight position away from the body. It is the opposite of flexion.

Flexion—The action of bending a limb, generally toward the body.

Gluteal Muscles—The three muscles that form the buttocks region, the gluteus maximus, gluteus medius, and gluteus minimus, which extend, abduct, and rotate the thigh.

Imprint—When the pelvis is tilted toward the nose and the lower back is flat against the floor to protect the back. It is used if the transverse abdominis is not strong or the legs are being lifted during an exercise. Also, people with back conditions such as spondylolysis or spondylolisthesis should imprint their backs and avoid back extension exercises such as Swan or Swimming.

Kinesthesia—The ability to perceive the extent, direction, and weight of movement without visual cues. This can be impaired after surgery or while taking medications.

Latissimus Dorsi—Broad muscle that begins in the back and ends under the arm that is responsible for helping you push up from a chair. This muscle may be tight after surgery.

Lateral Flexion—Side bending of a body part away from the body when facing forward.

Lymphatic System—The system including all of the structures involved in bringing lymph from the tissues to the bloodstream.

Lymphedema—Swelling attributable to the obstruction, damage, or removal of lymph nodes or other parts of the lymphatic system.

Neuromuscular—Concerning both nerves and muscles.

Neutral—The position of your pelvis when it is perpendicular to the floor when either seated or standing, or parallel to the floor when lying down. Your back should not be arched either forward or backward when in this position.

Parasympathetic—The system responsible for slowing the heart rate and decreasing sweating through vasodilation of the blood vessels. This is the system that we want to activate during Pilates.

Pectoralis Major—One of the two muscles in the front part of the chest that draws the arms closer, forward, and downward. It is important to stretch this muscle after surgery.

Pectoralis Minor—A muscle beneath the pectoralis major that extends to the scapula in the back. It lowers the scapula and depresses the shoulder joint.

Proprioception—One's innate awareness of posture, movement, and changes in equilibrium in relation to the body that is not dependent on visual cues.

Protraction—Drawing forward of a part of the body, such as the scapulae (shoulder blades) when you reach to hug someone.

Prone—To lie with the body face down.

Retraction—Pulling back a part of the body, such as the scapulae (shoulder blades), when you pull an object toward you.

Rhomboids—Muscles that retract or move the scapulae (shoulder blades) back when pulling back with your arms.

Rotator Cuff—Muscles that surround the scapula (shoulder blade) and keep the shoulder secure in the socket.

Serratus Anterior—Muscle that helps you protract or bring your arms forward.

Scapula—Shoulder blade.

Sympathetic Nervous System—A large part of the autonomic nervous system that controls involuntary muscles such as the heart and glands.

Supine—To lie with the body face up.

Transverse Abdominis—The deep abdominal muscle that we want to activate during Pilates by breathing. It helps to stabilize the trunk.

Thoracic Duct—The main lymph duct of the body that originates by the abdomen. It receives lymph from all parts of the body except for the right side of the head, neck, and thorax and right upper extremity. We want to activate this duct during Pilates through deep breathing and activation of the transverse abdominis.

Bibliography

Aaronson N. "Movement Toward Healing," *Advance for Occupational Therapy Practitioners* 2008;24(9): 48–9.

Abramowski MC. "Chemotherapy: Induced Neuropathic Pain," *Journal of the Advanced Practitioner in Oncology* 2010;1: 279–83.

Ahles TA, Root, JC. "Cancer and Cancer Treatment Associated Cognitive change-An Update of the State of the Science," *Journal of Clinical Oncology* 2012;30: 3675–86.

Ahles TA, Saykin AJ. "The Relationship of APOE Genotype to Neuropsychological Performance in Long Term Cancer Survivors Treated With Standard Dose Chemotherapy," *Psycho Oncology* 2003; 12: 612–19.

Aisha D, Alderman AK. "Review of Abdominal Wall Function Following Abdominal Flaps for Post Mastectomy Breast Reconstruction," *Annals of Plastic Surgery* 2009;63(2): 222–30.

American Cancer Society website: www.acs.org

American Cancer Society. What Is Bone Metastasis? www.cancer .org/treatment/understandingyourdiagnosis/bonemetastasis/bone-metastasis-what-is-bone-mets

Asher A. "Cognitive Dysfunction Among Cancer Survivors." *American Journal of Physical Medicine Rehabilitation* 2011;5(Suppl 1): S16–26.

Bason RH. "Eighteen Sensations after Breast Cancer Surgery: A Five Year Comparison of Sentinel Lymph Node Biopsy and Axillary Lymph Node Dissection." *Annals of surgical oncology* 2007;14(5): 1653–61.

Berger AM, Abernathy AP, Atkinson A, et al. "Cancer Related Fatigue." *Journal of the National Comprehensive Cancer Network* 2010;8(8): 904–31.

Bergman, A et al. "Incidence and Risk Factors for Axillary Web Syndrome after Breast Cancer." *Breast Cancer Research Treatment* 2012;131(2): 987–92.

Betz S. *Modifying Pilates for Clients with Osteoporosis.* www .therapilates.com/PDF/modifyingpilates.pdf

Brigham and Womens Hospital, Department of Rehabilitative Services. DIEP/SGAP Flap Patient Education. Boston, MA: Author, 2007. www.brighamandwomens.org/Departments_and_Services/surgery/ services/surgicaloncology/Images/DIEP-SGAP_patient_education.pdf.

Burt J, White G. *Lymphedema: A Breast Cancer Patients Guide to Prevention and Healing.* Alameda, CA: Hunter House, 2006.

Casley-Smith JR, Casley-Smith JR. *Modern Treatment for Lymphedema*. 5th ed. Victoria, Australia: The Lymphology Association of Australia, 1997.

Chen Z, et al. "Fracture Risk among Breast Cancer Survivors." *Archives of Internal Medicine* 2005;165: 552–58.

Courneya K, McNeely M. "Exercise During Cancer Treatment". Indianapolis, IN: American College of Sports Medicine, 2012. www.acsm.org/access-public-information/articles/2012/01/12/exercise-during-cancer-treatment

Cramp T, Bryron-Daniel J. "Exercise for the Management of Cancer Related Fatigue in Adults. " *Cochrane Database System Rev* 2012;2: 11CD008145.

Emery K, De Serres SJ, et al. "The Effects of a Pilates Training Program on Arm-Trunk Posture and Movement." Clinical Biomechanics 2010; 25(2): 124–30.

Eyigor S, Karapolat H, et al. "Effects of Pilates Exercises on Functional Capacity, Flexibility, Fatigue, Depression and Quality of Life in Female Breast Cancer Patients: A Randomized Study." *European Journal of Physical and Rehabilitation Medicine* 2010;46(4): 481–87.

Gambino D. *Age Perfected Pilates: Mat Exercises Designed to Improve Posture, Strength & Movement*. Minneapolis, MN: Orthopedic Physical Therapy Products, 2007.

Ganz P A, Kwan L, et al. "Cognitive Complaints After Breast Cancer Treatment: Examining the Relationship With Neuropsychological Test Performance." *Journal of the National Cancer Institute* 2013;105(11): 791–801.

Harris SR, et al. "Clinical Practice Guidelines for Breast Cancer Rehabilitation: *Syntheses of Guideline Recommendations and Qualitative Appraisals.*" *Cancer* 2012;118(Suppl 8): 2312–24.

Hayes SC., et al "Lymphedema After Breast Cancer;Incidence, Risk Factors, and Effect on Upper Body Function." *Journal of Clinical Oncology* 2008;26(21): 3536–42.

Hayes SC., Johansson K, et al. "Upper Body Morbidity after Breast Cancer: Incidence and Evidence for Evaluation, Prevention and Management within a Prospective Surveillance Model of Care." *Cancer* 2012;118(Suppl 8): 2237–49.

Keays K, Harris S, et al. "Effects of Pilates Exercises on Shoulder Range of Motion, Pain, Mood and Upper Extremity Function in Women Living with Breast Cancer: A Pilot Study." *Physical Therapy* 2008; 88(4): 494–510.

Kepics J. "Physical Therapy Treatment of Axillary Web Syndrome." *Rehabilitation Oncology* 2004;22: 21–22.

Komer SG. How Does Your Body Weight Affect Your Breast Cancer Risk? ww5.komen.org/ContentSimpleLeft.aspx?id=19327353541.

Kübler-Ross E. *On Death and Dying*. Scribner. New York, NY: Scribner, 2003.

Lee SA, Kang JY, et al. "Effects of a Scapula-Oriented Shoulder Exercise Programme on Upper Limb Dysfunction in Breast Cancer Survivors: A Randomized Controlled Pilot Study." *Clinical Rehabilitation* 2010; 24(7): 600–13.

Leidenius M, Leppanen E, et al. "Motion Restriction and Axillary Web Syndrome After Sentinel Node Biopsy and Axillary Clearance in Breast Cancer." *American Journal of Surgery* 2003;185(2): 127–30.

Levangie PK, Santaiser, AM, et al. "A Qualitative Assessment of Upper Quarter Dysfunction Reported by Physical Therapists Treated for Breast Cancer or Treating Breast Cancer Sequelae." *Support Care Cancer* 2011;19(9): 1367–78.

McAnaw M, Harris K. "The Role of Physical Therapy in the Rehabilitation of Patients with Mastectomy and Breast Reconstruction." *Breast Disease* 16 (2002): 163–74.

McNeely ML, Campbell K., et al. "Exercise Interventions for Upper Limb Dysfunction Due to Breast Cancer Treatment." *Cochrane Database System Review* 2010;6: CD005211.

Myers JS. "Chemotherapy-Related Cognitive Impairement: The Breast Cancer Experience." *Oncology Nursing Forum* 2012;39(1): E31–40.

National Cancer Institute website: www.nci.org

National Lymphedema Network. *Exercise* (position statement). San Francisco, CA: National Lymphedema Network, 2011. www .lymphnet.org

National Lymphedema Network. *Lymphedema Risk Reduction Practices*. (position statement) San Francisco, CA: National Lymphedema Network, 2008. www.lymphnet.org/pdfDocs/nlnriskreduction.pdf

Peppone LJ, Mustian KM, et al. "Bone Health Issues in Breast Cancer Survivors: A Medicare Current Beneficiary Survey study." *Support Care Cancer* 2014;22: 245–51.

Rock CL, Doyle C, et al. "Nutrition and Physical Activity Guidelines for Cancer Survivors." *CA: A Cancer Journal for Clinicians* 2012;62(4): 242–74.

Schmitz KH. "Weightlifting and Lymphedema: Clearing Up Misconceptions." *Lymph* Link *Article Reprint* 2010;22(2). www.lymphnet .org/pdfDocs/Weight LE Misconception.pdf

Schmitz KH. "Weight Lifting for Women at Risk for Breast Cancer Related Lymphedema: A Randomized Trial." *Journal of the American Medical Association* 2010;304(24): 2699–705.

Schmitz KH, et al. "Prospective Surveillance and Management of Cardio Toxicity and Health in Breast Cancer Survivors." *Cancer* 2012;118(Suppl 8): 2270–76.

Schmitz KH, Speck RM, et al. "Prevalence of Breast Cancer Sequelae Over 6 Years of Follow-Up: The Pulling Through Study." *Cancer* 2012;118(Suppl 8): 2217–25.

Schmitz KH, Courneya KS, Matthews C, et al. "American College of Sports Medicine Roundtable on Exercise Guidelines for Cancer Survivors." *Medical Science and Sports Exercise* 2010;42(7): 1409–26.

Smith E, Smith K. *Pilates for Rehabilitation: A guidebook to Integrating Pilates in Patient Care.* Minneapolis, MN: Orthopedic Physical Therapy Products, 2005.

StepUp-SpeakOut *Breast Cancer-Related Lymphedema: Essential Knowledge.* New Canaan, CT: StepUp-SpeakOut Inc, Revised March 2013. www.stepup-speakout.org

St John N. *Mat 1 Pilates Instructor Training Manual* (rev.). Sacramento, CA: Balanced Body Pilates Teacher Training, 2009. www .pilatescorecenter.com/index.php/teacher-training/balanced-body-pilates-instruction-certification.

Stan DL, et al. "Pilates for Breast Cancer Survivors." *Clinical Journal of Nursing Volume* 2012;16(2): 131–41.

Stubblefield MD, McNeely ML, et al. "A Prospective Surveillance Model for Physical Rehab of Women With Breast Cancer: Chemotherapy Induced Peripheral Neuropathy." *Cancer* 2012;118(Suppl 8): 2250–60.

Stumm D. *Recovering from Breast Surgery: Exercises to Strengthen Your Body and Relieve Pain.* Alameda, CA: Hunter House Publishers, 1995.

Wampler MA, Hamolsky D, et al. "Case Report: Painful Peripheral Neuropathy Following Treatment with Docetaxel for Breast Cancer." *Clinical Journal of Oncology Nursing* 2005;9(2): 189–93.

Wefel JS, Saleeba AK, et al. "Acute and Late Cognitive Dysfunction Associated with Chemotherapy in Women with Breast Cancer." *Cancer* 2010;116(14): 3348–56.

Weis J. "Cancer Related Fatigue: Prevalence, Assessment, and Treatment Strategies." *Expert Review of Pharmacoeconomics Outcomes Research* 2011;11(4): 441–46.

Winters-Stone KM, Schwartz AL, et al. "A Prospective Model of Care for Breast Cancer Rehabilitation: Bone Health and Arthalgias." *Cancer* 2012;118(Suppl 8): 2288–98.

Wyrick SL, et al. "Physical Therapy May Promote Resolution of Lymphatic Cording in Breast Cancer Survivors." Accessed on redOrbit.com, July 23, 2008. www.redorbit.com/news/health/517635/physical_therapy_may_promote_resolution_of_lymphatic_coding_in_breast

Resources

General

Academy of Lymphatic Studies
www.acols.com
Lymphedema resources

All 4 One Alliance
www.all4onealliance.com
Lymphedema garments financial assistance program

American Cancer Society
www.cancer.org
  cancer resources, stress management
  www.cancer.org/treatment/treatmentsandsideeffects/
  emotionalsideeffects/copingwithcancerineverydaylife/
  coping-with-cancer-in-everyday-life-toc

American Institute for Cancer Research
www.aicr.org
Nutritional information for cancer survivors

American Occupational Therapy Association
www.aota.org
How occupational therapy can help

Annie Appleseed Project
www.annieappleseedproject.org
Alternative therapies for cancer

Breast Cancer Freebies
www.breastcancerfreebies.com
Hundreds of free products for breast cancer patients including wigs,
  prosthetics, and retreats

Breast Reconstruction.org
www.breastreconstruction.org
Educational website on breast reconstruction

cancer101.org/toolkit/order-navigator
Planner to be used both during and after treatment to keep track of
  treatment and response

Cancer Care
www.cancercare.org
Financial resources

Cancer Information Service
www.cancer.gov/aboutnci/cis
Evidence based cancer information

Cancer Survivors
www.cancersurvivors.org
Cancer information, resources, and support

Cleaning for a Reason
www.cleaningforareason.org
Free household help

Cook for Your Life
www.cookforyourlife.org
Teaches healthy cooking to cancer survivors

Happy Chemo
www.happychemo.com
Discounts for cancer-related products

Heal a Woman to Heal a Nation, Inc.
www.hwhn.org
Promotes life-long learning and holistic wellness for women and girls

Living Beyond Breast Cancer
www.breastcancer.org
Great informational site

Look Good, Feel Better
http://lookgoodfeelbetter.com
Free cosmetics and hairstyling information for cancer survivors

Lymphnotes
www.lymphnotes.com
Lymphedema information

Meals to Heal
http://meals-to-heal.com
Home delivery of nutritious meals

Medscape
www.medscape.com
Latest information on cancer

National Cancer Institute
www.cancer.gov
Research-based information on cancer

National Library of Medicine
www.nlm.nih.gov
World's largest biomedical library

National Lymphedema Network
www.lymphnet.org
Lymphedema resources

National Women's Health Information Center
www.womenshealth.gov
Women's health information

National Women's Health Network
https://nwhn.org
Women's health activists

Pink Fund
http://thepinkfund.org
Short term financial aid during treatment

Step up, Speak Out
www.stepup-speakout.org
Lymphedema information

Triage Cancer
www.triagecancer.org
Navigating cancer resources

The Wellness Community
www.thewellnesscommunity.org
Classes and programs for cancer survivors

Clothing and Lymphedema Garments

Bright Life Direct
www.brightlifedirect.com
Latex free lymphedema products

Confident Clothing Company
www.confidentclothingcompany.com
Fashion conscious therapeutic clothing

JANAC
www.janacsportswear.ca
Bras and sportswear

JUZO
www.juzousa.com
Compression sleeves

Lymphedivas

www.lymphedivas.com

www.lymphedivas.com
Lymphedema gauntlets and sleeves with style

Shop Well with You
www.shopwellwithyou.org
Body image resources for women surviving cancer

Softee USA
www.softeeusa.com
Prosthetic garments and camisoles

Equipment Vendors

North Coast Medical
www.ncmedical.com
Equipment such as raised toilet seats, dressing aids, bathroom equipment can be purchased here

Apps

All of these Apps can be downloaded to the iPhone. Please check for other operating systems. Most of these are free.

BMI (Body Mass Index) Calculator
There is a direct correlation between BMI and cancer reoccurrence risk, so it is important to know what it is and if you have to reduce yours.

Computer Ergonomics
Suggestions to help you at your desk when working with a computer

iChemodiary
For chemotherapy management

iEat for Life
Nutritional tips and meal suggestions

iHealthlog
Tracks appointments, test results, lab values and weight

iPharmacy Drug Guide
Identifies prescription drugs and side effects

Med Helper Pro
Keeps track of appointments and multiple health conditions

My Fitness Pal
Helps you with your fitness and diet goals

My Med Lists
You can update your medications and have them readily available

My Pearl Point Cancer Side Effects Helper App
List of side effects and evidence-based information on management

Pill Reminder
Helps you to remember to take your pills

Pills On the Go
Keeps track of your medications

Relax Melodies
Songs that you can play during the day to relax your mind and body

Stretch Break
Reminds you to take a break and stretch daily

Index

About the Authors

Naomi Aaronson, MA, OTR/L, CHT, CPI, CET

Naomi Aaronson is a nationally known author, speaker, and occupational therapist who specializes in breast cancer rehabilitation using Pilates. She is a certified cancer exercise trainer as well as a certified mat Pilates instructor. She has provided workshops for Primacare, NE Seminars, Integrated Rehab and Fitness, Brick Bodies, and to graduate occupational therapy students.

As coauthor of the learning CDs *Return to Life: Breast Cancer Recovery Using Pilates* and *Breast Cancer Recovery: On Land and In Water*, Aaronson seeks to educate both survivors and health professionals throughout the world about the importance of rehabilitation in survivorship after breast cancer. Her motto is "take back your body and improve your physical and mental health after cancer." She lives in Bayside, New York, and in her free time, enjoys Pilates, reading, traveling, and spending time with her cat.

For more information, please visit her website at www.recovercises forwellness.com.

Ann Marie Turo, OTR/L

Ann Marie Turo is an occupational therapist, author, and lecturer on the use of Pilates with breast cancer patients. She has devoted her 30+ years as an occupational therapist to helping her patients lead healthier and more productive lives through her practice Integrated Mind and Body, LLC, where she works with all ages from pediatric to geriatric. During her breast cancer treatment, Turo started her Pilates reformer training. Currently, she is fully certified in STOTT Pilates® from Merrithew Health and Fitness™ in Mat, Reformer, Cadillac, Chair, and Barrels. In addition, Turo is a certified yoga and tai chi instructor and Reiki Master who believes in the power of using an integrated approach to rehabilitation.

Turo lives in Boston with her husband Arthur and enjoys reading, practicing yoga, and knitting for family, friends, and charities.

To learn more please visit her website at www.integratedmindandbody .com.